Bible Belt Queers

Love + Revolution

Edited by Darci McFarland

Cover designed by Iris Gottlieb
www.irisgottlieb.com

Copyright © 2019 Darci McFarland
All rights reserved

Acknowledgements

Thank you to the countless people who have been part of bringing this book to life.

Thank you to all of the talented contributors who answered the call for submissions. Thank you for raising your voices to show the world that we're here, and we're queer - even in the South.

Thank you to Zoie McNeill for your help proofing the collection for printing. Thank you to our cover artist Iris Gottlieb for the beautiful cover design.

Thank you to my patient and brilliant partner, Elia, for always listening to my process and supporting my work. I love you, and I appreciate you so much.

Thank you to my LGBTQIA+ chosen family scattered all over Arkansas, Oklahoma, Texas, and Tennessee. I am forever inspired by your strength, love, and resilience.

Thank you to my mom, Candace, for being the best parent I could have ever hoped for. Thank you for your continuous support and encouragement. Thank you for being the love and care I needed. Thank you, thank you, thank you for being a safe haven for this bible belt queer.

Table of Contents

Introduction by Darci McFarland………………………………………………...8
Do They Know by Blake Haney…………………………………………………9
Love a Sinner by Bee L. Buchanan……………………………………...…10-12
Flag'n 4 #homespunqueers by (Gina) Mamone……………………………13
on Things that should have Freed me. by Kyle Medlin……………………14-15
Exodus by Shannon Novak……………………………………………...16-17
the ten commandments and how to break them by Cassie Anders………….18-19
Good Ol' Boys by Basil Soper……………………………………………….20
Pure Pleasure (Chippewa Falls, WI) by Michael Borowski……………………21
Silver Rhymes with Darkness by Rebekah Morgan…………………….....22-24
A Blessed New Experience by Antonia Terrazas………………………….....25
How I Got to Memphis by Joey Thibeault………………………………...26-27
A Creation Story by SK Groll…………………………………………….28-30
farm home refuge by K. Cox………………………………………………31-33
Between Shadows by Rachel Trusty……………………………………….34
Love Thy Painter by Erin Grauel……………………………………….35-41
American Queer by Brianna Peterson……………………………………...42
Daughter, Son, Child by Mary Scales English……………………………43-44
Wanderer by micah clark…………………………………………………45-46
Clear Creek by Mikey Walden……………………………………………….47
Summer '18 by Mikey Walden……………………………………………...48-49
my queerness resists by Soph Bee………………………………………….50-51
Bashback! Possoms by Chelsea Dobert-Kehn………………………………52
Corpus by Jeffery Smeal……………………………………………….53-59
it was never about the house by Oliver McKeon……………………………60-62
Love in the Arcade by Rachel Trusty……………………………………….63

Life Left Unsaid by Cheyenne Brown..64-71
Of All Things by Kate Ericksen..72
Womb to Womb by Sterling Bentley...73-74
I'm Afraid of Snow by Kenna Lindsay...75
Untitled by Darci McFarland..76
Gran'mama Died Before I Was Gay Hannah Cather.............................77-78
These Mountains Run Deep by Lucy Parks...79-84
What Am I Going To Tell My Mother by Kenna Lindsay......................85-86
This is Me by Mary Beth Breshears..87
Show Me Yours by Mary Beth Breshears..88
absolution by Kat R. Vann..89-91
The Moon Beneath Her Feet by Donald Neel......................................92
Sheep by Marion Rose Young..93-94
Thibodaux Pink Sky by Elias Capello..95-100
elephant in your cupboard by Kat R. Vann.......................................101-102
Bless the hushed mouths by Cristina Dominguez..............................103-106
Make a Joyful Noise Unto the Lord by Ayden Love.............................107
Lift Up Your Heart Unto the Lord by Ayden Love...............................108
HOLY, gospel by Ayden Love..109
Glory to God in the Highest by Ayden Love.......................................110
HUMAN by Elizabeth Lawrence...111-112
Staying Safe by Jordan Venditelli...113-115
Queer Little Wonders by Flannery Quinn...116
Madam and Eve Leeanne Maxey..117
Where I Come From by Caroline Earleywine.....................................118
Proverbs by emet ezell...119-120
I Gotta Ask by Zion McThomas..121
The Growing Season by Kelly Ann Graff...122

Jesus Saves by Caleb Matthews..123-126

Look Me in the Eyes by Shana Carroll...127

When It Comes to My Parents, I'm a Secret Agent by Shane Allison...........128

Still Valid by Nour Hantouli...129

Bent & Broken by Sterling Bentley..130

Quilted Queer by Amanda Balltrip..131

Lavender by Hannah Elizabeth Seiler...132-133

A Woman Looking by Peri Drury..134-136

Wet by Layla Padgett..137

rubyfruit by Lauren Beard..138-139

Return to Church by Peri Drury...140-141

Gran'mama Died Before I Was Gay by Hannah Cather............................142

Please Open Your Hymnals by Kelsie Fitzpatrick....................................143

Thoughts and Prayers Leeanne Maxey..144

Her vs. Him by Nyna Nickelson..145

Queer Foot First by Haden Leevi...146-148

Cuntry Flag'n by (Gina) Mamone..149

How to Become by Eryn Brothers..150-160

On the last Sunday of September by Fernande Galindo......................161-164

Open Relationship by Shannon Novak...165

Eulogy for Gomer by Dawn Betts-Green..166-167

A Tourist by Zoie McNeill...168

The Choice by Leeanne Maxey...169

Penance by Emma Fredrick..170

My Only Sin is Being A Woman by Briheda Haylock..............................171

Bless Your Heart by Heather Stout..172-174

God's Plan by Ty Little...175-176

Home by Taylor Allison...177

A Family Legacy by Darci McFarland……………………………………....178

Trinity by Layla Padgett………………………………………………….179

Ransom Note by Luce Grace Kokenge Hartsock……………………….....180

A Texas Drag King's Gender Delight by Theodore Vegas Zydeco Longlois……………………………………………………………...181-183

Dolly the Shepherd by Chelsea Dobert-Kehn……………………………184

Swallowing Light - Mick McClelland……………………………….185-189

Genderless Angels by Hayden Dansky……………………………….190-194

Grounded/Burning by Klée Schell………………………………………...195

God's Perfect Will by Antonia Terrazas………………………………….196

Battle Scars by Haden Leevi…………………………………………197-207

For my grandmother by Dartricia Walker………………………………...208

Wish You Were Queer by Sarah Meng…………………………………...209

The Choices I Make by Leah Whitehead…………………………….210-217

Contours by Jean Thomas……………………………………………218-221

Confessions of a Pentecostal Queer by Amanda L. Pumphrey….…...…222-225

Community by Darci McFarland………………………………….....226-228

[Content Warning: The work in this book could be triggering as it contains discussions of violence, loss, homophobia, transphobia, and other traumatic experiences.]

Introduction

Being Southern is so many things.

It's sitting between rows of strawberries, picking the best and brightest to eat as your great grandma yells "get out of them strawberries!" and your great grandpa yells back, "You leave her alone! She can eat as many of those strawberries as she wants!"

It's pulling honeysuckles from the vine as you daydream in the yard because "the day is too nice for you kids to be in the house!"

Or fishin' for craw-dads in the creek behind your cousins' house.

It's summers spent swimming at the lake.

Living off popsicles and dodging fireworks shot by your brothers like your life depends on it, because your life probably depended on it.

It's sunburns, sunflower seeds, and baseball games.

No stop lights in those small towns.

Certainly no queers.

Because they're all goin' to hell for their sinful lifestyle.

> so we stuff our differences down
>
> deep inside ourselves
>
> and plot our escapes
>
> bury ourselves in books
>
> and wait.

Being queer and Southern is wraught with tension. It takes some of us years, decades, lifetimes to shed the shame woven into the fabric of who we are. Some of us never do.

It's knowing too many of us who didn't make it.

This book is for them too.

Do They Know?

Do they know?
Crabapple trees standing in a backyard not my own.
Just by the way the words tumble out of my mouth?
Rotting fruit not fit to eat.
Twigs make for good houses and bridges.
Tree trunks make for good home bases.
Sisters have crushes,
And I have crushes on their crushes.
Do they know?
Pine needles cover the floor of the woods,
Cover my tracks that I was looking in the window
Hoping he was coming to play or changing shirts.
Don't change pitch unless it's lower.
Clip my *sssss*
Dogwood tree's beautiful punishment striped red across my legs.
Do they know?
Do I sound...
My words betray me when I was taught they would help the world understand me.
Tulips mom planted covered in cement by the city.
Tulips mom planted pushing through cement the next spring.
Do they know?

- Blake Haney

Love a Sinner

"How do you love a sinner, but hate the sin?"

I am ten, sitting in the van with my mom, the fabric seat hot under me and the Alabama August sun.

Mom gives it some thought, her hands clutching at the wheel, while I sit on mine, nervously .

"Why do you ask?" I hear part curiosity, part suspicion in her voice.

"Uncle Elijah."

Uncle Elijah is gay.

This is something my family talks around, but never targets.

"I love your Uncle Elijah," Mom says after a moment. "But what he does, how he lives, that's sin."

I know what she means, but I still don't understand. Sin and sinners are intertwined, so much a part of each other.

Later, I am twenty, visiting Mom's family. We learn that my uncle's most recent partner has contracted Hep C.

"That's what he gets, for living this lifestyle," Mom says casually. For being gay, she doesn't say. For being a sinner.

I hate it. "Love the sinner."

Sin isn't some amorphous blob, attaching to people and drastically changing their bodies. Even my mother believes in original sin. The bottom line: you are human; you are a sinner.

"Love the sinner," is never said about the neighbors, because we Southerners use "bless your heart" to patch up that hole. It's only sin; sinner when it comes to something truly outrageous.

Then, I am thirty, and I fall in love with a girl.

She is awkward and kind, dark hair and darker eyes, and a wide smile, and she makes my heart race.

I am only human when faced with such beauty.

So, I am a sinner.

Perhaps it is the unapologetic nature of being gay that makes Christians hate it. Unashamed about loving one another. They don't ask for forgiveness for something Paul said in his letter to the Romans. Or other cherry picked lines from the good book.

I prayed so many times for normalcy; that my desires were okay.

I never once asked for forgiveness.

As I grew to realize that some part of me was vastly different than those surrounding me, I prayed instead for virtues. For patience, love, and understanding. This humanity, this love in me shouldn't be inherently shameful.

Shame like when you've broken the antique knick knack you're great grandmother passed down, and then lied about it.

Because it's not an action, it's being. So when the preacher says homosexuality is wrong with such conviction, like saying the sky is blue, I felt fear. I felt shame.

But that broken knick knack feeling never comes.

Unapologetic.

Yes, the sky is blue.

But in the morning, the Alabama sun paints the sky pink and gold and purple.

And I am only human when faced with such beauty.

- Bee L. Buchanan

Flag'n 4 #homespunqueers by (Gina) Mamone

[Image Description: This image is a digital art illustration of a granny square quilt flagging in blue jeans.]

on Things that should have Freed me.
By Kyle Medlin

On any given day with the most common place verbiage, I am gay. Plot twist, most days I don't want to be. It's funny how things that are supported as positive engagements can still be negative predicaments. Watching movies about love usually makes me sad - to use common place verbiage. To use uncommon place verbiage, it makes me feel topsy turvy. A blender of desires, fantasy, and shame turns all my colors brown, a mixture of what this world expects me to find joy in on a canvas of what the church says is right.

I'm realizing that life is a lot more than just a coloring book page with four crayons.

It's funny how joy can make you feel so depressed sometimes. When I get happy drunk - I lock myself in the bathroom, I don't want to privilege myself with desirable things, a mirage of this reality. Dating apps are the positive, the platter of socially acceptable pornography - a positive engagement. Each night is a reminder that no one is beside me. Each morning, I'm hoping to surprise the sun with a lover -

The secret is I am ambidextrous - I can only write with my right hand but my heart only swipes left.

Both sides of this earth speak of freedom - either in acceptance or denial and every day gravity is crushing me in between two opposites, each claiming freedom.

I didn't know feeling free would be this heavy.
I didn't know I would make it this far and still be confused.
I don't know how long any of this is going to last
- maybe that's the scary part.

Sometimes I get brave- I DM someone with symphonies of attraction hoping to teach them a song that I've prepared for someone - anyone. I've been rejected every time. I've been told that this makes me a bad Christian, and I've been told this makes me a bad gay person. Some other times I get brave, tell people of my love of myself apart from sexuality, tell of untold divine mysteries. I'd delete all my apps and feel full. I've fallen short every time. I've been told this makes me a bad Christian; I've been told this makes me a bad gay person.

Fun fact: I didn't know it was going to be this hard to be bad at so many things. In sports they bench you for not being talented, in class they don't call on you even if you know what's right; in life, well, let's just say I've run out of pieces for people to shame me for having.

I wish I had something empowering to say.
I wish I had someone empowering to be;
I've been told it's a powerful statement to be single, but to me it just feels more brave.

Dear past self, I'm really tired of being brave.
Dear future self, I've been really brave, and its tiring.
Dear present self; I was hoping by this point that someone else would have told you you were worth being around by now.
And I'm proud of you for doing your best to say it every day.

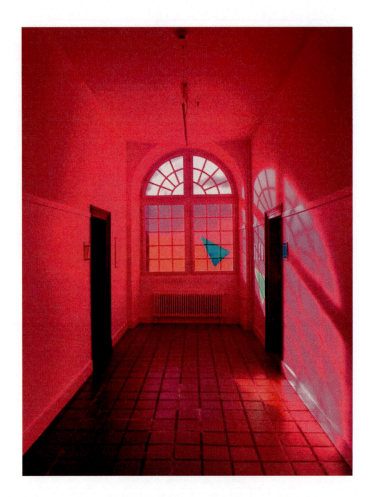

Exodus by Shannon Novak

[Image description: This work represents the healing and breaking free from conversion therapy. Transparent pink vinyl is applied to the windows in an old hospital hallway, flooding the space with intense pink light. One of the windows has a cerulean isosceles triangle in the middle on an angle. The triangle represents the body (or person) breaking free from the darkness into the warmth and acceptance of the queer community. Music sheets are installed on the wall to the right of the windows - the song "Blackbird" by the Beatles.]

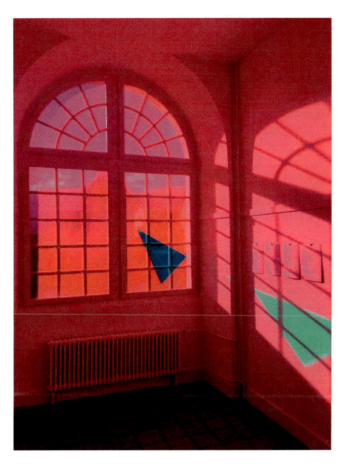

Exodus by Shannon Novak

[Image description: This work represents the healing and breaking free from conversion therapy. Transparent pink vinyl is applied to the windows in an old hospital hallway, flooding the space with intense pink light. One of the windows has a cerulean isosceles triangle in the middle on an angle. The triangle represents the body (or person) breaking free from the darkness into the warmth and acceptance of the queer community. Music sheets are installed on the wall to the right of the windows - the song "Blackbird" by the Beatles.]

the ten commandments and how to break them
By Cassie Anders

when we were six we sat in hard plastic chairs around a table just our size, with pigtails and pleated dresses and shiny patent leather mary janes over lacy little socks. we learned about the ten commandments and how to be good in words that we didn't yet know how to read.

i. you shall have no other gods before me.

when i was seven, anne shirley and laura ingalls and lucy pevensie seemed a lot kinder and more powerful and more worthy of adoration than the god i kept hearing about in sunday school. i snuck a book inside my bible and spent sunday morning with harriet the spy.

ii. you shall not make for yourself a carved image…you shall not bow down to them and serve them, for i the lord your god am a jealous god.

when i was eight i kept a world map on my bedroom wall and spent more hours dreaming about the world i wanted to see than i ever spent in prayer.

iii. you shall not take the name of the lord your god in vain.

when i was nine i told my family that god had been working in me and that i was ready to be baptized. i told the preacher i was saved. i didn't tell anybody that i only did it to stop the uncomfortable questions about whether or not i had accepted jesus into my heart.

iv. remember the sabbath day, to keep it holy.

when i was ten my mother told me that i was too old to lay down across the pew and nap during church. pay attention, she said. you're a christian now, act like one.

v. honor your father and your mother, that your days may be long in the land that the lord your god is giving you.

when i was eleven i wondered if the reason i wanted to die was because i wasn't honoring my parents enough.

vi. you shall not murder.

when i was twelve i let my mom take me to get my eyebrows waxed, and my hair layered, and she told me how pretty and grown up i looked. i wondered how ugly i had been before.

vii. you shall not commit adultery.

when i was thirteen i kissed a boy who was seventeen and he put his hands up my shirt. i didn't know why i was afraid to tell him to stop.

viii. you shall not steal.

when i was fourteen my boyfriend snuck a pack of cigarettes away from his older brother and we smoked one behind the gym. he coughed and spluttered and said never again. i took another drag.

ix. you shall not bear false witness.

when i was fifteen i put on more eyeliner and wore tighter clothes and felt uglier every day.

x. you shall not covet anything that is your neighbor's.

when i was sixteen my best friend got a serious boyfriend and i spent the entire year ignoring the real reason i hated him.

Good Ol' Boys

Traveling towards obligation the day before Thanksgiving.

Swollen clouds are grey and pink.

Watch for falling boulders.

We stop at gas stations,
there are no pieces of our people. Billboards papier-mâché the road, still no pieces.

We find pieces in an iPod.
We find pieces in our intertwined hairy knuckles.
We find pieces in the mountains that we threaten to abandon.

We drive
further into
the bible
belt, only
hoping to
unbuckle it

with our teeth.
- Basil Soper

Pure Pleasure (Chippewa Falls, WI) by Michael Borowski

[Image description: An adult video store in a grass field at dusk. The pink neon sign reads "Pure Pleasure." To the right is a flag pole with an America flag and a variable message sign reading "24 HOURS."]

Silver Rhymes With Darkness
By Rebekah Morgan

I was heading down 421 N. towards West Virginia about to hit the Tennessee border near Tater Hill, and I saw clouds crest then drop over the mountain side and crash down into the town like a wave.

I saw a dead possum in the road freshly eviscerated by a raven and more American flags flying at half mast then I could pitch a flame at.

The man on the radio talked about the local teenage football stars. He talked about momentum and about all those boys getting ready to play in the rain and the snow this evening, and the snow fell on my windshield like some sort of wind whipped dandruff.

I passed by Borderline Fireworks coming into Tennessee, and I received an Amber Alert on my cell phone reporting about a beige Honda Odyssey. I switch dipped a hairpin past Cherry Springs and continued north through High Country past the antiques and primitive shop and a little gas station called DNB mini market that promised the freshest gizzards around.

The road signs along this stretch of highway are mostly unrelated to driving. There are signs about upcoming shooting matches and wrestling matches and tractor pulls and signs warning about various animals that might block your way along this stretch of road.

I drove by an old silo with a sign out front that said BJ's Treasure Shop, and I nodded my head at that mess. I kept on driving, and I saw a little cabin with a blue tin roof, and I thought it was the most beautiful cabin I'd ever seen and that blue tin roof reminded me of the ocean.

The fog surrounded me in Tennessee, and I thought something like, 'wow this is one hell of a fishbowl,' as I passed Mike's B-B-Q Pit entering into Mountain City.

I passed by Sherry's chicken house and on the other side of the road there was a mountain somebody had blown the top off of. Somebody had scraped it down it's sides, and it nearly broke my heart in two.

The sun didn't come out going around Maple Bend, but the hundreds of-years-old barn up on the hillside was some sort of beacon of light in and of itself and I felt good about being on the road.

I hopped on 81 N. near the Iron Skillet in Virginia, and the rain started coming down a lot harder the second I got on the interstate. Red truck flew up behind me fast, and I said "God damn!" out loud to my can of Monster energy.

I got up to the Grayson Highlands near Marion, and there wasn't shit to look at besides semi trucks and power lines and bright orange trees split open like sweet potatoes. I'm exactly 100 miles from Beckley, West Virginia, and I feel more awake than ever.

I crossed Route 666 over Hogback Road and nearly swerved off the road trying to text my sweetie about how much I loved him. The trees on the side of the highway were mangled into huge burley masses, and it looked like the whole entire Forest has been burnt down at some point.

That "Knocking on Heaven's Door" song came on the radio, and I quickly changed it because I don't want no fucking bad omens on this trip. I don't want no bad omens ever. I don't need that bad juju in my life anymore, and I quit listening to Led Zeppelin and Pink Floyd and all that bullshit a long time ago. Nothing good comes from listening to that type of shit, just bad omens and fucking staircases to heaven that you aren't ready to climb. Sometimes your friends climb those fucking staircases too early, and it's real sad to watch them go, and I feel like there's some kind of magic power in changing this radio station, so I'll don't get vexed by the bullshit.

"Come on Eileen" came on the next station, and that was much more fitting, and that was a much better sign. I passed a Bojangles, and I thought about getting a biscuit, but I don't think I have time for biscuits. I never know if I have all the time in the world or not. I wonder if anyone ever fucking knows what time it is anyway.

I paid a two dollar toll with mostly pennies off the floor and drove through the big Walker Mountain Tunnel. The orange lights illuminated everything around me, and it was like driving through the sun.

I passed by The South Gap on my way towards Bluefield and all the clouds came down off the hillsides and touched the ground. It seemed unnecessary, but it was nice, and I felt like I was swimming while I passed mile marker 63. I watched a silver laced boulder roll down off the side of the mountain crash down into a guardrail, and it didn't phase me one bit.

I passed through the tunnel going under East River Mountain, and I noticed the sun was still out inside of that tunnel. The radio cut off, and I went real deep into that tunnel. Looked like it was going to go on forever, some sort of matrix shit. It was real beautiful, and I really do love driving through the underbellies of these mountains. Someone drilled a hole straight through the mountain like it needed an asshole.

I have to pee so bad coming out the other side of the tunnel it's like the world is going to end. I'm 45 miles to Beckley, and I'm 1 mile to Bluefield. This is what happens when you cross into wild and wonderful West Virginia. The trees have color again: red, yellow, and orange. It's like some giants holding out a bouquet of mums. The wind is blowing real crazy, my cars moving side to side coming through this mountain pass, and I ain't stopping to piss.

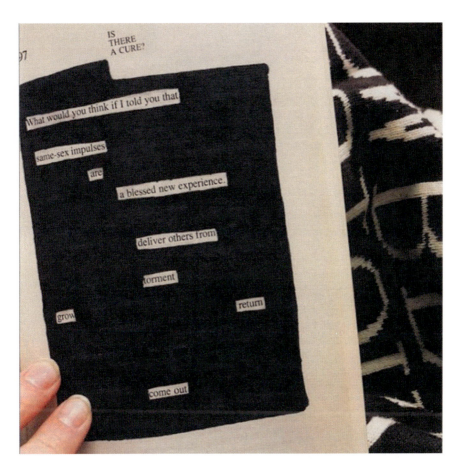

A Blessed New Experience by Antonia Terrazas
Original text from "The Unhappy Gays" by Tim Lahaye.

[Image Description: A book open to a page of text that has been mostly crossed out in black marker, revealing a found poem that reads, "Is There a Cure? / What would you think if I told you that / same sex impulses are a blessed new experience / deliver others from torment / grow / return/ come out."]

Cecil, Horseshoe Lake by Joey Thibeault

[Image description: A photograph of Cecil, illuminated by the light streaming through a window in an abandoned fishing cabin on Horseshoe Lake, AR.]

Harvest by Joey Thibeault

[Image description: Photograph of Cecil T Brown I, uproots a cotton plant in Tunica, MS as the sun sets behind cumulus clouds.]

Cotton boles by Joey Thibeault

[Image description: Photograph of Cecil T Brown I splaying open a defoliate cotton bole to check for insects.]

Mississippi is Burning by Joey Thibeault

[Image description: Photograph of Cecil looking over burning soybean fields in Tunica, MS. After harvest the stalks are burnt to release nitrogen back into the soil.]

A CREATION STORY

i.
this story does not start (or end) with
the sad not-girl & the dog on a mountain

        still alive & not sure what is next.

this story did not begin with the not-girl
or the dog. or even the mountain.

        this story begins with god.

ii.
god said *let there be a canyon*
    & the earth split itself
    down the middle

god said *let there be a daughter*
    & my mother split herself
    in two

god said *honey make your mother proud*
    i picked up the wood-axe to build a fire
    & split myself at the elbows

        god weeps.
        she didn't
        mean it
        like that.

god says *promise me you'll be safe.*
    i built you the sturdiest body:

    just like mine.
    i am so proud of the

    [woman] you've become
    i don't mind the axe. the static. the elbows.
    your body was not the first thing i made.
    i started with the canyon. then the mountain.

    then the sky. then you. everything else
    that came after, i built to keep you safe.

god asks *sweet [girl]*
    why are you crying?

    i have tears enough to grow this world again
    & again- my rain will come when you need it.

    save your sorrows for the world. the daughter. the life you will create.

iii.
i am
so sorry,
[mom]

you made
the whole
world
for me

& i keep

splitting my-
self into
anything but
the daughter
you planned for.

    -    SK Groll

farm   home   refuge

twenty-five mile long drive
from neighborhood with yards,
skating sidewalks, pool party friends,
was C's house : farm home refuge.

flower beds. pastures. toy tractor.
horizon lines. mudroom. barncats.
black fences. dirt and soil.
the sound of bacon frying. 2 eggs. 1 powdered donut.

wheels became my own
adolescent freedom
I would drive backroad kentucky scenic byway
to C's house.

three hours north to college
far enough away / close enough to return
farm   home   refuge
turned walking on land
after she died
becoming ritual practice
visiting ancestors
hearing messages

i have only just begun.

twenty years no longer C's house
remnants of her history still alive in
bottom dresser drawers. costume pendants. leather gloves.
back closet hanging blazers. hat mannequins.
woven blankets, stained quilts. half century old faded sheets.

i slowly shave her scent
carrying odor and place packed
car door to door

bloomington. chicago. durham
now, country newfound :
queer   farm   home   refuge

this last peeling of hers
a most precious gift :
frayed primary blue bunny and flower blanket
covers my legs warm
family china, engraved parfait glasses
floral sheets so faint and soft
i envelop myself or
tuck in the sides
sound of bacon frying. 2 eggs. 1 powdered donut

making beds

as she did

stewarding her spells

here

queer

farm home refuge.

- K. Cox

Between Shadows by Rachel Trusty

[Image description: Ink and hand-embroidery on a found photograph of two girls sit in the grass under a tree and look at the camera. Both girls have short brown hair in a bob hairstyle. The girl on the left is wearing a bright yellow dress with a blue belt. The yellow dress has white polka dots on it. The dots are embroidered onto the photograph creating a texture. The girl on the left with the yellow dress has her arms around the girl on the right. The girl on the right is wearing a brown dress. They are surrounded by yellow-green grass. A farmhouse and more trees sit behind them. A blue sky peeps through breaks in the trees. The leaves of the trees have been embroidered onto the photograph.]

Love Thy Painter
By Erin Grauel

      My days in the summer of 2016 were all about working myself until exhaustion. Even after doing physical labor from sun-up to sundown, I didn't sleep well. I moved back to my hometown of Myrtle Beach, South Carolina the summer previous after an eight-year stint in New Orleans. The reasons behind my move were varied, but it was mostly to be closer to family. The culture shock of moving from a city as liberal as New Orleans to a decidedly more conservative beach town was expected, but what I didn't expect was Donald Trump's presidential run. And not just that he was running, but that he was winning.

      People in my hometown lauded the angry man spewing vitriol on television and through his decidedly not presidential Twitter account. He tapped into their fears, stoked them, invented them in some cases, and then promised it was he and only he who could fix them. I thought, and I suppose many people thought, if Hillary Clinton kept making sense, kept being an unflappable politician, eventually Trump would wear himself out. But as the summer progressed it was becoming clear that no matter what monstrous things he did or said, the man could do no wrong with his supporters.

      I worked as a painter and as a maintenance person that summer. Most days I wore a baseball cap, paint covered jeans and a t-shirt. It started to feel like maybe I was being stared at, or more likely scowled at whenever I was in public. If I stopped in the grocery store or at a restaurant on the way home from work, I could feel people double-taking me. Wondering why I dressed so boyishly. Why my hair was cut so short. I couldn't decide if it was in my head or not until I got a job with my father painting the interior of a Baptist church. It was then when I realized just how big the culture gap was between me and the rest of my town.

      Neither my father nor I are religious but he got the job painting the church because my nieces and nephews attended its daycare. At least once a day Carol, the daycare director and the woman managing the painting project for the church, would ask us which church we went to and why didn't we join theirs. Dad would lie and say he went to the Methodist church near his house. I would say I didn't attend church. This line of questioning was innocuous enough, I suppose, but it didn't end there. It seemed every day a wandering Baptist would approach me and question why I wasn't fitting into society as they understood it. I was a single thirty-two-year-old childless woman doing general labor, and the church folks could not fathom how I could find happiness in any part of that scenario.

Carol was a short, wide woman with a loud voice. She was a person who saw something that could be improved in everything. And then would point it out. And then have someone else fix it. She was a master delegator and appreciated my father's ability to carry out her plans without complaint. Her sidekick was the church's music director, Jack. He fit the stereotype of many church music directors—married to a woman and with a child, but flamboyantly gay acting (effeminate mannerisms and speech, impeccable dresser, hair coifed and gelled into a Ken-like pompadour). He was great at picking out paint colors and envisioning design ideas. He and Carol both took on the project, not only of redesigning the church, but also of interrogating me about my life.

On my third day of work Carol approached me as I crouched to paint a baseboard in one of the church's offices.

"Can I ask you something, sweetheart?" she drawled, her head cocked to the side as she stared down at me.

"Sure." I smiled up at her.

"How old are you?"

I held my smile. Thirty-two.

"Well. Are you married?"

I laughed. Mostly because I wanted to immediately shout "I'm gay!" and have the whole conversation end. Instead, my goofy grin held, and I told her no. This was not good enough for Carol.

"Do you have a boyfriend?" She continued trying to make her voice sound sweet and soft.

My dad was in the room, and I could feel him cringing. I considered telling her about my on again, off again relationship with a genderqueer experimental theater artist. I had been sexting with them mere moments before this conversation. But I was afraid my dad might lose the contract if the church found out his helper was a homo. A homo actively sending gay texts into the church's airwaves. I paused and said "No, I don't have a boyfriend."

"Well, I can't believe that," Carol scoffed. "We need to find you a boyfriend. A good one. Don't we, Cliff?" she said looking to my father who was making a not so stealthy exit. My dad knows I'm gay, but it's not something we talk about. Even if I was straight it wouldn't be something we talked about. He certainly doesn't discuss relationships with my straight sisters either. He gave a curt "hmm" and then pulled out his tape measure and pretended there was something he needed to size up in another room.

Jack too, was very interested in my relationship status.

"You're single?" he asked me one day. "And you're how old! Amber, why?" (He liked to call me Amber even though that is not my name. I'm not sure why he found it so hilarious to call me the wrong name. But it was amusing to hear him say "Aaaammmberrrr" in his thick effeminate southern drawl, so I went with it.) My reaction to these questions was a shrug and a coy smile. I didn't have it in me to fight back. Gay or straight, the questions were ridiculous. No one needed to be married anymore. My sexuality was always on the tip of my tongue though. I wanted to see how they would react to finding out about my queerness. But then the economics of it would wash over me, and I would remember something in another room that needed to be re-measured.

One day Jack and Carol approached me as I climbed a ladder to remove a broken ceiling tile.

"Amber," Jack started.

"Amber? Why do you call her Amber?" Carol chastised.

"Because. She looks like an Amber."

"No, she doesn't. She doesn't even have red hair."

"Well I don't know. Don't question me. I just do, Carol. She doesn't mind. Do you Amber?"

"No, I don't mind," I said staring down at them, struggling not to roll my eyes at how little they knew of me. "Call me whatever."

"See?" Jack said. "Anyway. Amber. How old are you?"

"Thirty-two," I repeated for the I don't know how manyeth time.

"Oh," they both said in disappointed unison.

Then Jack continued. "We had someone we wanted to set you up with. But you're too old."

I wanted to meet the poor, young, inevitably also gay boy they thought I should date. I didn't ask more questions though. I didn't want to encourage this behavior.

Later that week Carol confronted my mother, as she took my nieces and nephews to the church's daycare, about my singledom.

"Kathy," she said. "Erin is how old? And she's not married?" My mom laughed.

"Well, we need to help her," Carol insisted, "Find her a man."

My mom's response was to shrug and say, "Hey, if it ain't broke, don't fix it."

I liked that response. I didn't particularly want to be single. Or in an on again off again relationship with an experimental theater artist who sometimes loved me and sometimes seemed to forget I existed. I did want a partner. Someday, maybe. Just not on the terms Carol and Jack seemed to think I needed.

One day one of the women who worked in the church's front office approached my father and me while we were moving furniture out of one of the rooms to be painted.

"Oh, you are so strong," she said to me as I helped my dad lift a desk.

I did my typical response. Smile and laugh. I knew this comment was going to lead somewhere uncomfortable. Then she turned to my father.

"God didn't bless you with any boys?"

"What?" my father responded.

My father is hard of hearing but this summer I hoped his constantly asking people to repeat themselves was a tactic. A way to make them uncomfortable for asking such nosy and odd questions.

"A son," the woman persisted, "You've got your girl working for you, but God didn't bless you with boys?"

I wondered if she thought Dad had made me a spinster by allowing me to work for him.

"I have a son," my dad said. And then we continued working and ignoring her. I have an older half-brother living in Maryland who fights addiction and is often unable to work. He and his current wife often crash with his ex-wife and her new husband. The church lady's attempt at finding a more "normal" arrangement for my father was not working.

I also changed air filters in condos that summer. My mother is the maintenance manager of a condo rental company and got me the gig. She also does not fit into traditional gender roles. She has short hair and dresses boyishly. She can fix and build things as well as my father. But because she is married to him, she is allowed to pass. No one asks her questions about her personal life. Changing air filters was a task that had to be performed once a month, and I always looked forward to filter changing week because it meant I got a break from working alongside my father in a stifling church all day. The condo rental company had approximately three hundred units that needed filters changed. I drove a large white work van and hauled boxes of clean filters into, and then boxes of dirty filters out of, countless high-rise condos occupied by tourists. I was paid by the filter so it was in my interest to get the task done as quickly as possible. I wore a cap, t-shirt, shorts, sneakers, and a carabiner filled with keys on my belt. In my rush up and down elevators, back and forth across streets, in and out of condo units, I often felt more thing than human. A sweaty creature working for money, working to achieve exhaustion.

Most of the time when I knocked on condo doors no one answered. The occupants were down enjoying the beach. I would use my keys to let myself in, race to the closet where the air conditioner was, pull out the dusty old filter, throw in the new one, and jet back out before anyone even knew I was there. I was always a little afraid entering the condos that someone would be lurking. I had walked in on more than a few people napping on the couch or sitting at the kitchen table thinking they could just ignore the knocking and shouts of maintenance at their door. It was also always on my mind that someone in the condos might pull a gun on me. These were paranoid times, and the condos were occupied by anxious people who watched Fox News all day. This is not hyperbole. In just about every condo I went into, that's where the television was tuned. To a "news" program constantly heralding the end of the world at the hands of liberals and minorities.

Even after video footage leaked of Donald Trump bragging about grabbing women by the pussy, his supporters would not be distracted from their end goal of Trump in the White House. The day after the video was released, I overheard a man in a restaurant say loudly and without reservation into his phone of Hillary Clinton, "They should cut her tongue out, string her up, and then do worse to her." I understood why Donald Trump's fear tactics were so effective. Because now I was so afraid of his supporters I was checking my passport expiration dates and considering buying a taser. (As an aside, my mom did buy me a taser for Christmas that year, which I subsequently lost, along with my vibrator in a move. I hope whoever found that box was able to put them both to good use. Maybe even at the same time?)

In one instance, after doing my routine of knocking on the door, shouting maintenance, knocking again, shouting again, and then finally resorting to letting myself in, I was greeted by a family sitting slack-jawed at the kitchen table eating lunch. There were two women and a few kids. "Oh," I apologized. "I knocked and shouted. I'm here to change your air filter." Then I held up the air filter. The family continued to stare. The television was on, and I could hear a Fox News anchor bashing Hillary Clinton.

"Okay," I said, "so I'm just going to change this filter then."

I turned to go to the AC closet. One of the kids at the table hopped up and went into the bedroom. As I kneeled to change the filter, I felt someone looming. It was what the child had hopped up to fetch. Over me was a man with a mustache and shaggy hair. I repeated my story about how I had come to be in his condo while I hurriedly finished changing the filter. I stood up to face the man who looked about to shake with rage.

"This is unacceptable." he said

"I'm sorry?" I answered

"No, this is crazy. You can't just walk in here unannounced."

I wanted to point out again just how announced my visit was. Not only because of my yell knock yell knock routine but also because the renters are told at check in that someone will be coming around to change filters.

"I need you to get out of here right now." he said. "I am not happy about this. People can't just come in my house."

He stood inches from my face. This was the kind of man who carries a gun, I thought. This is the kind of man who would have shot me without pause and then blamed me for making him do it. This was a man living a life of fear and paranoia. This was a man defending his family from a threat that didn't exist. I left the condo, walked to my work van, and decided to quit while I was alive for the day.

The next day I was on edge as I began my work changing filters. I was terrified I would walk in on another ill-prepared family. At one of the first units I went to, the door was answered by a young man in a short robe.

"Oh, hi!" he chirped, "I love your top."

I looked down. I was wearing a navy blue polo shirt which I was already sweating through.

"Uh, thanks," I mumbled. I held up the air filter in my hand. "Mind if I change your filter?"

"Oh, no! Come on in." He stepped aside for me. Inside the floor was littered with bits of rainbow confetti. There was champagne in a bucket on the table and a banner across one of the bedroom doors declaring "Congratulations, Steve."

"We had a little celebration last night," the man told me. "My boyfriend got his doctorate."

"That's wonderful!" I gushed.

"Want some champagne?" he offered, raising an eyebrow at me.

I wanted to say yes. He was the only person who had ever offered me anything in my rush from condo to condo. I wanted to spend the morning with him and his doctor boyfriend and not watch Fox News and not talk about why I didn't have a boyfriend.

"I'd love to, but I have to get back to it."

The man winked at me and said, "Oh, alright then. You have a good day, sister."

I wanted to cry and hug him. Instead, I walked back out into the heat and tried to prepare for what might be behind the next door.

American Queer by Brianna Peterson

[Image Description: American Queer is a mixed-media piece created with watercolor, color pencil, and coffee on paper. In the foreground are two female figures standing shoulder to shoulder. The female on the right is wearing overalls, holding a beer in her left hand, and her expression is a playful pose. The female figure on the left is slightly shorter. She is wearing a dress and holding a broom. Their props serve as parody to heterosexual gender norms within relationships. In the middle ground behind the two figures, there is a vintage pull behind RV trailer. Two plastic yard flamingos are planted in the ground at the door of the RV trailer. The setting is outdoors in a grassy field. In the background, nature is further depicted by trees that exists on the horizon line to create a forest.]

Daughter, Son, Child

I am a daughter of these
        mountain hollers.
    I am a ridge runner.
        A chaser of the sun,
            and a lover of the night sky.
You showed me what love
        through Christ was,
    But I rejected it.
        You showed me what hate
           through Christ was.

        I rejected that too.

I am a son of rising peaks.
        Rough and craggy,
    You shaped my soul.
        You taught me that thriving
            can happen at Breathless elevation.
 I am a rider of the
        high wind. A chaser
    of snowflakes on frozen lands.

        You showed me compassion.

I am a child of the
        Earth.

Landscapes reflected on tattooed skin.
  My inheritance tied to the ground
    on which
      I stand, I reconciled myself.
To duality.
     The Deep South within me,
     but only a foundation -

For growth, evolution into truth.

- Mary Scales English

Wanderer

Christ was an opportunity to learn
        s e l f l o a t h i n g
when you are trans
& southern
& poor
salvation looks more like

sleeping through the night
and less like altar prostration

truth be told
baptism
was simply coercion into drowning
in a sea of
        "your misery is divine ordination"
      "this agony is all apart of the grand design"
            "the devil will be on your heels now,

                                        g i r l."

if Christ could have *struck down* the
        constant demons of my own devices
if Christ could have *stayed*
        the hand of violence against my body
if Christ could have *silenced*
        all tongues of knives
            from his own herd

            maybe I would have believed
      but miracles are the ghosts of David's bones

            and I am a *Moses*

                        of my body
                        of my gender
                        of my people

                              & of my faith.

how much longer
must this body wander
before I truly know who I am.

      - micah clark

nitrogen fixation+oxidative phosphorylation+sweat+shit=Nature. Nature is God. maybe God is Math. sometimes being clean—washing the Earth off of my body—feels like an abomination. or maybe it just feels that my body is. my body is God? my body is the Devil. in the image of sweat and shit—deer hide stretched, scraped clean. dust-coated skin reminds me where i've come from (where i'll go) caught in the interstitial space of bedrock and mountaintops. my body is an abomination, my body is sacred, a temple, holy,   my body is the Devil?   my body is God.

Clear Creek by Mikey Walden

[Image Description: First panel is the text "What I'd think of this body" over a person, nude, sitting in a creek cupping water in their hands. Second panel is the text "if this body were mine" over the same person, nude, sitting in a creek washing mud off their face. Below both is the text: "Nitrogen fixation plus oxidative phosphorylation plus sweat plus shit equals Nature. Nature is God. Maybe God is Math. Sometimes being clean—washing the Earth off of my body—feels like an abomination. or maybe it just feels that my body is. My body is God? My body is the devil. In the image of sweat and shit—deer hide stretched, scraped clean. Dust-coated skin reminds me of where I've come from (where I'll go) caught in the interstitial space of bedrock and mountaintops. My body is an abomination, my body is sacred, a temple, holy…my body is the devil? My body is God."]

Summer '18

i am so infatuated with far-off things—
the city and Saturn and my future self—
my
(lungs full of air)

self
(whoosh out)

tickling the inner surface of my abdomen with fingertips drenched in never-enough
as i age in fluorescent lights that work like my mind—
discolor my face
disphorize the future

and i'm getting ahead of myself—
i'm so far from where i am—
i'm so sorry
to so many versions of myself
that all fit like socks that got mixed in with my laundry
squishing my toes
or the heel pulled up on my achilles.

to my selves:
i figured it out!
i'm nothing i thought i was
and everything i knew i was.

and so i hope from the bottom of the central time zone
that whatever i feel in this moment
and all the moments following it like an anxious friend
feel right
so i can float on it
lungs full of air—
whoosh out—
pull it back in—
kick your feet—
still on top
and let it dry on my skin in the sun, edged with a gentle white crust
to wear the lines it gives my body with self-assuredness
like sneakers that keep my feet planted firmly
and a bandanna that keeps my hair out of my eyes.

- Mikey Walden

my queerness resists

my queerness is me, my love,
freshly washed sheets on the bed
and Bob's Burgers on TV.
my queerness loves her
kalamata olive eyes
and the tattoos that ink her skin.
my queerness is sparklers in my belly
when she looks at me and
fireworks when I kiss her
my queerness worships the way
she makes every moment a celebration.
but my queerness does not always live
and breathe in this utopia.
my queerness sees your dirty looks,
your male gaze, your smacking lips.
my queerness knows you wish it were
a whisper and shouts anyways.
my queerness spits at your
"who wears the pants?"
my queerness swallows the punchline
before you finish your joke.
my queerness knows you think it is
a product to be bought and sold
but it is not a commodity.
my queerness glares at the
rainbow flags in store windows,

their logo smiling proudly from the fabric
my queerness resists the urge to hide
from the police at the pride parade.
my queerness resists the tears
that want to pour on Sunday mornings
my queerness resists
my queerness can be blood boiling,
fist clenching, voice raging -
but all of the time, it is flowers.
it is a beautiful thing
that spent years growing through dirt,
blooming unapologetically
in the garden of myself.
my queerness wants to dance.
my queerness holds her hand in public
and does not tremble.
my queerness traded its fear
for a baseball bat.
my queerness wants you to know
that it struggled and fought its way
towards a battle cry *pride*,
and it will never
be forced into silence
again.
- Soph Bee

Bashback! Possoms by Chelsea Dobert-Kehn
Digital collage for Fistmas, Queer Appalachia's holiday campaign. Dec. 2018.

[Image Description: A gang of opossums with pink bandannas over the lower half of their faces are gathered at the North Pole. Hand-made pink signs they display mimic signs from Bashback! Actions: "These faggots kill fascists", "No pride in corporate greed".]

CORPUS
J. Peter Smeal

You and Me. We were brothers.

We were brothers to our families, who first made the joke.
We were brothers to the people we repeated it to like gospel.
We were brothers and we knew it, like we knew dirt was red, tea was sweet, and Mama's love was forever.
Twins, born exactly the same from the toes on our flat feet to the tops of our towheads.
    Only three weeks apart...
        ...and to different parents.

    But brothers just the same.

My mother dreamed your birth like Old Testament prophecy.
In a room filled with gauze and light she saw your mother laid out on a table before a great window.
Her hair - Bible black and already ankle long - pooled around her in impossible abundance, spilling over the table edge in ribbons of rilling jet fringe. The light teemed through the glass over her body and her massive belly glowed full of it.
Inside, in shadow, was a butterbean of a boy with a full head of straw hair and his father's nose.

It was no surprise when she awoke to a ringing phone heralding your arrival.
It was no more of a surprise when, twenty-one days later, a second call from your mother presaged that my own emergence was nigh.

The day we first shared a crib they found us holding hands, and from then on we loved each other with an intensity that belied our blood.
    We were brothers.

Then one day, we were eight. Resting in the porch shade after playing in the yard

all morning, I wickedly lifted my bare, dust caked foot to your face and dared you to kiss it.
To my great surprise, you leaned forward and placed your lips on the place my arch should have been and pulled away with a loud smack.
You swore and spat and wiped your lips on the hem of your shirt.
Then, with a smile full of the devil you dared me, in turn, to kiss the neighbor's monstrous, foul tempered German Shepherd square on his black wet nose.

That dog's name was Bear.
Later, at the emergency room, that fact caused a small ruckus among the nurses
~"...*a **WHAT** bit you?"*

Only seven stitches that day, but a permanent sneer of a scar for the rest of them.
I've had to drape it behind moustache since my first pubertal whisps.
I never blamed you, though.
I never blamed you for anything.
 -The mouthful of wasps
        -The pellet in my leg
                -The little knot on my occipital bone
                        -The yellow pine branch under my kneecap
                                -The green slivers of coke bottle in my eye.
They are trophies... souvenirs...the inheritance bequeathed us by our past.

The sons (and often, daughters) of the pissant towns of the backwater South bear a particular sort of willfully arrogant ignorance toward gravity and its consequences.
Keloided limbs flailing, bursa snapping like bubble gum, shattered wrecks of smiles under retinas flapping like window shades - we toss our tender selves into, against, and through our fragile youths. Most of those fortunate to reach maturity intact have x-ray roadmaps with hairline filigree to trace the journey.
It is a drive so deep it's almost genetic; to not simply ascend the peak of the steep roof, but to then - hammer in hand - dance on the rain slick shingles.

It was, in fact, that same spirit - that celebration of unfettered physicality - we were honoring three years later when your mother discovered us naked in my bedroom.

We'd had enough of a beating from the summer sun and retreated to my room at the back of the house where the trees hung thicker. After pulling blinds and cutting lights, we punched the old window unit awake and teased its buttons and knobs until it growled and spat onto the carpet. It wheezed and sliced the soupy air with ice and we peeled out of our sopping shorts and wrestled for prime seating.

We cackled at the farting sound the beanbag chair made against our bare butts. We summoned glorious flatulent croaks from our armpits when our chilled drying rumps failed to produce them any longer then sniffed at our fingers for the new salty smell we found there. Finally, tiring of the curious silliness of being in bodies that had odors and made noises, we draped sheet capes over our shoulders and watched *The Great Space Coaster* at high volume while rubbing our goose-pimpled arms, cheek-by-cheek on the floor.
When you mother cracked the door to call us to lunch, that's how she found us.

Is it time and age or the terror of that moment and the shock of what followed that colors my memory of her gasp? In my mind it seems impossibly, inhumanly loud and long for a single breath - even one powerful enough to pull all the joy from that room with it.

The door crashed open, and as she descended upon us, we scattered.
Catching you in her fist, her carefully coiled bun shook as she fought to hold you then exploded into a curtain of black that twitched and reared around you both. In the flickering half light from the television, I couldn't make sense of the dark undulating shape of your struggle.
As you lurched and reared closer to where I cowered, I tensed, ready to break and run.
Then some part of your confusion of limbs caught the edge of the blinds and tore them, clattering, from the window. Uncaged, the sun pounced through the glass and wrapped itself around you, setting you aflame. The sudden light struck me like a bolt that took my sense and pinned me to the spot.

As my eyes adjusted, I knelt on the floor in a panic fugue and watched while she broke her hand beating you in front of me.

My stomach rolled as you squealed and pleaded. This unjust violence did not happen in my home and I hung transfixed between indignation and the impotence of a 'good boy'.

You hung from her fist by your elbow, dancing on your toes as you hopped and twisted away from her blows. She swatted in time to a howling chant, punctuating each connection with a word: "Jesus Does NOT Like THAT! Jesus Does Not LIKE That!..." on and on.

I had looked at your body almost as often and as curiously as my own. I had curled against it in sleep, bathed with it, embraced, marked and laid innocent hands and eyes on it in a thousand ways.

Now, in the alchemy of fear and outrage and confusion, this strike of radiance sparked inside me and I saw.

I saw how the summer sun had baked you lean and brown as the lizards under the porch - all dry, whip-quick angles.

I saw how you had condensed and, under a residual layer of baby fat, showed the first signs of powerful arches and sweeping valleys to come.

I saw, as my eyes swept up the tense comma of your torso, the ladder of your ribs and gentle peaks of your chest, across the widening triangle of your back and up your arm to your wrist where your mother's hand gripped like knotted rope.

I saw the cruel cables in her arm tensed to the sharp peaks of her shoulders as they pulled the thin fabric of her nightgown and rose under her skin like breaching whales.

I saw down the hard crooked branch of her other arm and now to the offending hand, open and bent back on itself against the resistance of the air as she whipped it at your skin. Full circle as she made contact, the press and jiggle of your flesh and pink ghosts of fingers blurring into welts of red.

I saw, even in that moment of ugly ignorance, how gracefully the knots of her knuckles swept down into the cords and hollows of her wrists to the dancing slopes and crests of her forearms.

I saw the crimson twist of your ear diminish at its lobe to a tail of freckles turning back around your neck to disperse across your shoulders like a dusky sky of dark stars.

I saw the hard little crabapples at her jaw, anchoring the flat sails framing the soft hollow of her throat.

I saw the balance and pull of tendons taut as D strings where your calves pushed your feet into arcs below and pulled open the secret smile at the cups of your knees.

She stopped with a final guttural cry, and the curl of your body hung from her, tense with pain and shame but submissive and resigned. I took you in, blissed with terror, and the tableau brought to my mind a picture in a book, terrible and beautiful in luminous light, that I half remembered from a room that smelled like butter cookies and crayons and tweed hot from a sunny window.

I let out a gasp of my own then, I think.
And I said something like, "oh"
While inside I was crying
"Oh! Do you see...? Do you SEE?"

If I'd known then it was a question I'd be asking the rest of my life, known that the line of bodies down the thread of my days would all connect back to this revelation, that every blush and ecstatic sigh, every bit of flesh I took on, around and into my own was a passionate communion with this moment of exquisite pain, I might have said it out loud.

You would not look at me but I couldn't turn away from your hot-from-crying face. I longed and despaired for you to meet my eyes. I ached to snatch at your retreat, to pull you back to me with my gaze and with every nuance I could conjure in it say "I see you. I know you. I love you". But if you had looked, I wonder, would you have seen instead only where I had broken open… where plates shifting along my mantle sent a new ocean surging between us.

I know you never forgave me for escaping my own beating. When she released you,
she declined to spank me. Turned up her nose like I was too filthy to touch... though I could see her holding her hand behind her back as her adrenaline passed away to blooming pain.
Instead she said that my parents would "take care of me" when they got home.

We all knew better, of course.
My parents were tacit nudists. They had no particular philosophy on the topic other than the practical notion that clothing was mostly a social nicety. After crossing one's own threshold, it could be cast off as though on fire. Don't get me wrong, we were decent people, just not above answering the door in our underwear.
My Mom, having no place in her home for that kind of shame, just called her an "Ignorant fool".

You though… did you blame me? Did you remember that it was my idea? We never *ever* said a word about it between us or even acknowledged that it happened.
Except that from that day on you would not even wear shorts or so much as take your shoes off in front of me.
And how could I answer to that with a mouth that still felt the chill of the cheek, frosted in the tv light, I had laid a quick dry kiss on only seconds before that door flew open?

Then the summer ended. Not long after, our fathers' business, friendship, and respective marriages fell apart.

Then one day I found myself kneeling against the hot back seat of our silver-blue Pontiac Bonneville, peering through the rear window at a yellow-gold Cadillac. Beyond that other window was a boy I could barely see through the reflection of the sky on the glass. But I knew he knelt too, staring back at me.

He raised his hand and I wagged mine so hard my wrist popped.

The taffy soft highway tugged at our tires as we pulled apart and I watched and watched until the heat shimmer rippled up over him, squeezed him flat then smeared him into the Mississippi blacktop.

Thirty years on and there are still you-shaped holes in me. Their edges are softer, vaguer now where time and my poking fingers have eaten at them.

But what remains, what always will remain…
       is the solid press of hard packed ground under my heels and red dust in my toes;
              the gamey smell of Bear's food on his breath
                    and the feel of your lips on the sole of my foot and
              how, even after the all day
                          sting of the sun baked clay, they burned there.

it was never about the house

in 2005
home was a little grey truck
with purple pinstripes
and a rear window
that didn't latch -
a fact that came in very handy
at least twice a week
when I left my keys in the ignition
(they were always
right where I left them -
I guess not many joyriders
know how to drive stick.)
the place I lived
was a big stucco house
with a cozy bed,
a fenced-in yard
for the dog to play in,
and an altar in the dining room
where queer sons could pray
to be delivered
from their sins.

in 2006
I left that big stucco
and home took me
all over the South -

to a house
on the edge of the suburbs
that always smelled of patchouli
(the kind of place
where you didn't have to wonder
if you were welcome,
acceptance never came
with a caveat,
and truth didn't require penance) -
to pride festivals
with more queer people
than I once believed existed
in the entire world -
to small-town gay bars
where fearless queens
showed me what it looks like
to defend your identity
as fiercely as you'd
defend your life,
because next time
it might be
the same fight.

years later,
long after I sold
that little grey truck
and went back
to that big stucco house

a little less angry
and a lot more myself,
years after I had
a house of my own,
home kept taking me
where it always has -
just a little bit farther from shame,
and just a little bit closer
to where the love is.

- Oliver G. McKeon

Love in the Arcade by Rachel Trusty

[Image description: Two women play a stand-up arcade game. The woman on the left is caucasian and is wearing a white shirt with horizontal pink stripes. She has on short, blue shorts. Her hair is pulled up in a loose bun. She appears to be actively playing the arcade game. The woman on the right stands slightly behind the woman on the left. She is African American. She is wearing a white tank top with pink striped shorts. The woman in the back has her left hand lovingly placed on the other woman's bottom while she watches the game. Two other stand-up arcade games can be seen behind them suggests they are in a larger arcade.]

Things Left Unsaid

By Cheyenne Brown

When I was a kid, I thought an electric shock could make someone gay. One hot summer afternoon, I knelt on the brown shag carpet of my great grandmother's home and popped a tape into the VHS rewinder. I held the electrical plug of the device in my hand and looked at the outlet. It was round, different from the other sockets in the house. I wasn't old enough to know the difference.

"Be careful," my grandmother warned me. "That's the outlet that electrocuted your cousin Mike and made him gay."

Something about my grandmother's caution caught me off guard. Of course, she was looking out for my safety by not wanting me to get shocked, but also it sounded like she didn't want me to become gay like my cousin. I didn't know what it meant to be gay. The only thing I knew for sure was that it meant people didn't like you.

"You still a faggot?" my grandfather would ask with a southern drawl when Cousin Mike visited for Thanksgiving. My cousin would get upset and storm out into the backyard while my grandfather chuckled. The words my family used to describe my cousin were foreign, but I felt an immense amount of empathy for him.

I took my grandmother's advice and stood up. I walked across the room to a different outlet and carefully connected the plug to the socket. I wish I could say that back then I felt something. Some sort of spark or jolt that could have verified the family mythology surrounding homosexuality, but I felt nothing. So often in my life it has felt as if others have wanted an answer when there isn't one.

The first time I recall recognizing the subject of my family's hatred, I was in the checkout line with my mother at Kroger. This grocery store was the bustling center of my hometown. Every afternoon, southern housewives would fill their carts with semi-fresh vegetables while making their way up and down the artificially lit aisles. My light-up tennis shoes squeaked on the freshly waxed linoleum floors. I couldn't have been older than seven or eight. Two women in their late twenties stood together in front of my mother and I, holding hands. I began to study them. Of course, as a young girl I would hold my friend's hand on the playground or as we'd cross the street. I never thought anything of it, but these women were different. I realized that I had never seen two adult women holding hands in this sort of way. I thought about what this action meant for a moment before I watched one of the women kiss the other on her cheek. The other woman laughed, and I felt the way I imagine some people do when the straight couple gets together at the end of a Nora Ephron movie.

"Excuse me," my mother loudly interrupted, "there are children here! Do not do that in front of my daughter!" I immediately felt anxious as I watched my mother cause a scene.

One of the women turned around, understandably upset, "Do what?"

"What you were just doing!"

"Why? Are you afraid that just seeing me kiss my girlfriend is going to make your daughter gay?"

It was a pointed question, and I wanted to cry. I felt like I'd been caught watching something on television that my mother didn't approve of. I diverted my eyes to the harsh glow of a refrigerator filled with Dr Peppers. I didn't want anyone to dislike me because I believed something about these women felt right. I was ashamed that my mother had verbally accosted them for a small expression of love. My stomach churned because I knew that identified with them somehow. I was afraid. I didn't know what any of it meant, really, but I thought I was wrong for feeling this way.

"Let's just go," the other woman said as she set down her basket of groceries. For a moment, I made eye contact with her, and I believe that we had the same expression on our faces. It was a look of apology, and we were both apologizing to each other on behalf of my mother.

I had just entered high school; my mother was driving, and I was sitting in the passenger seat of her blue sedan. We were stopped at an intersection, waiting for a tractor to turn left on to another farm road by our house. Some country song about a girl riding in a truck with her boyfriend was playing on the radio.

"You know," my mother turned off the music, "if I had a gay child, I'd kill it."

"What?" I managed to ask before my throat began to close. I looked out the window and averted my blushing cheeks. The song on the radio was about a straight couple, so why did this thought cross her mind? Was it because I had a poster of the blonde country singer in my bedroom? I felt caught, and I assumed she had found out about me. I wasn't even sure that I was a lesbian, so how did she know? I thought maybe I had forgotten to clear my search history on our home desktop computer. I would use AOL instant messenger to chat with my friends after school. We mostly talked about boy bands, and although I enjoyed the bubblegum pop, I wasn't on the same page when my friends called the gangly boys with fringed haircuts "hot." I began researching reasons why I might not like boys in the same ways that my friends did. I formed an idea that I had always suspected, but I was meticulous in covering up my tracks.

I kept thinking; was it that I hadn't taken a date to the school dance? In our group picture, my friends and I all stood on a dock by the lake. Every other girl leaned against her date, but I stood alone at the end of the line, gripping my sparkly clutch.

I rubbed my shaking hand against my red cheek. I wasn't wearing makeup. My mother always said that I looked "dykey" if I didn't wear makeup.

"At least put on some blush before we go out!" she'd say testily.

I knew what she meant—I didn't have that Dallas look. I didn't wake up at six AM before school to curl my hair and shade my eyelids. Her words stung, but there was something rebellious about not rolling a mascara wand across my eyelashes every morning. Still, I felt overwhelmed with guilt for something that she demanded I feel sorry for.

"I want you to come help with my presentation," my mother finally stated after not answering my question. I don't know what she knew back then or why she asked me to join her. All I knew was that I was afraid of my mother. I felt sick. She had been working on a *reparative therapy* study in her psych program at Texas A&M University. Homosexuality had been removed from the Diagnostic and Statistical Manual of Mental Disorders (DSM-II) in the seventies, but The American Psychiatric Association has yet to ban conversion, or reparative therapies. I tried ignoring the details of her research. I was afraid that if I asked questions I would come across as too curious and then I'd be shipped off to one of the camps or boarding schools my mother researched.

When most people think about conversion therapy, they think about the idea of "praying the gay away." Often this is correct, but there's an underlying pseudo-science to it as well. Sometimes I wish that I had been given this false information under religious pretenses because that would make more sense, but I wasn't. Religion was something I could laugh about. Academia; however, seemed much more credible. I had no reason to believe that some science or research could be less than truthful.

I followed my mother into a small lecture hall. She set her computer bag down and removed a chunky white MacBook. I sat down next to her, watching her pull up a PowerPoint. She walked over to the instructor and they chatted awhile before my mother put the presentation on a USB drive. She uploaded it to the PC in the classroom as seats began to fill.

I looked around at the students taking out their notebooks and writing down the title of the slide, "Sexual Orientation Can Change: Ending Same-Sex Attraction."

My mother began to explain how *homosexual* was a challenging word. Labeling one's self as gay, lesbian, or homosexual was as existential threat. If patients wanted to change, they shouldn't put themselves in a box, she said. There was no proof of a "gay gene" either, so there was no basis for someone having these attractions. Being gay was a choice.

My mother would glance at me as she lectured, and I'd sink further into the seat. I had been too scared to ever label myself. In my family, gay, lesbian, or homosexual was a slur. Why would I ever want to consider myself to be someone my family hated? I never thought about there being a "gay gene" either. If my sexuality was a choice, I couldn't remember making that decision.

I tensed a little bit and tried to straighten up my posture. I didn't want to draw attention to myself. I couldn't help but wonder if my mother had chosen this topic because of me. Was I the reason she was researching a way to "cure gays"? Were the pamphlets for different reparative therapy options for me?

My mother went on to explain that same-sex attraction was nothing more than a bad habit, and like all bad habits, it could be broken. It was only a matter of rewiring the brain through reparative therapy. Sometimes people had a weak masculine or feminine identity. I thought back to the many times when my mom called me a dyke. I didn't think I had a weak feminine identity, but maybe she thought I did. I dug my nails into my hands and tried to seem some version of normal.

Often, I have pondered what it means to have a "weak feminine identity." My father's nickname for me is Peppermint Patty, like the *Peanuts* character. Peppermint Patty's defining characteristics are that she likes sports, slacks off in school, and is close with her father. Popular culture usually insinuates that she is a lesbian. I never thought my father's pet name for me was backhanded per say, but I did wonder how he meant it. Within this past year, I asked my father.

"Don't be defensive," he laughed, "you seem annoyed with men."

When people ask my father why I'm not dating a man he usually smiles and says, "Well she's never had much interest in boys." The other person typically laughs and makes some remark about how I haven't found "the one" yet. After my mother's presentation, I tried my best to force myself to like men. After all, I only had *a bad habit that needed to be broken*. If my mother wanted me to change, I wanted to change for her. No matter how hard I tried; however, I couldn't will myself to like the opposite gender. And trust me, I tried.

In 2015, President Obama condemned therapies "repairing" gay, lesbian, and transgender youth. A decade after my mother's presentation, it was becoming commonly accepted that reparative and conversion therapies were nothing more than pseudoscience. By then, however, the damage had been done to thousands of LGBT youth. I am incredibly lucky that the looming threat of being sent away never came true, but I still believed everything she taught. I was immoral and it was my fault.

The summer before my twenty-fourth birthday, I was sitting with friends at a dive bar in the East Village of Manhattan. My father works in the music industry and has traveled between the West and East Coast for most of my life. I'll fly in to spend time with him and visit my friends that have relocated. The dark musty bar was empty considering we were out on a Sunday night. A couple of us were displaced Texans, so we shared spicy margaritas that reminded us of home. Jason, however, ordered a gin and tonic. He had curly hair and horn rimmed glasses that made him look like a caricature from a seventies comedy film.

"This bar is lame," He complained. "Why didn't we go somewhere with a rooftop?"

"I like it," I shrugged, looking around at the paneled walls covered with objects that reminded me of my grandfather's hunting ephemera.

I opened a text from a guy that I had been talking to ever since he messaged me on Instagram. He had recently graduated from Amherst, and it was unclear how he found my account. He had a Lou Reed cover band which sounded insufferable, and he mansplained Phillip Roth novels to me, but there was something entertaining about talking to him. Most days I ignored the guy, not because I didn't like talking to him, but because it felt a little bit like gonzo journalism. It felt nice to have someone care about me, and I knew my mother would like him, but it wasn't the right kind of attention that I wanted.

"What if I moved to Austin to be your boyfriend?" the guy from Amherst texted me.

"Yikes." I said, after reading his text aloud to my friends.

My friend Jason shrugged, "I don't get what's so bad about that."

"I'm gay." I laughed, realizing I had never admitted it out loud before. Although whether it was only because I was outside of the South was anyone's guess.

"Tell 'em that," our other friend replied bluntly.

"No, don't," Jason interrupted as if I was lying to the guy, "You're not a lesbian."

"Yes, I am," I said, shaking him off.

"You're just drunk."

I rolled my eyes, "I've had one margarita."

"I've known you for years," Jason said as if he had some sort of authority on the matter of my sexuality.

"I think I would know if I liked women."

Jason vaguely gestured at me, "but you don't look gay."

"What the fuck, Jason?" I asked, getting annoyed with his condemning tone. "I can't believe you just said that."

"I didn't mean it that way... I meant you don't have that dyke look," he said, his voice softer.

"I am a dyke, Jason!" I yelled, embarrassing him. I didn't care if he cowered at the same word he had just used a moment before. Six blocks from Christopher Street, the center of New York's LGBT community, nobody was likely to judge me for making this declaration.

At this point, the bartender, who had no choice but to listen to us, walked over and held up a bottle of vodka.

"Yeah, we need some of that," I nodded to the bartender as he lined up three shot glasses.

"Since when are you a lesbian?" Jason quizzed me.

"Since always," I said, taking a swig of the clear alcohol.

My father texted me declaring that it was too late to be out in the city alone. I explained that I wasn't really alone and some of my friends were from Texas. The L train stopped running, and I asked Jason to walk me back. I assumed that my father would feel better if I was in the presence of a guy instead of walking around the Village alone. I explained this to my father as her continued to send me multiple text messages. It was the first time that it occurred to me that at least one of my parents cared about me. I had never seen him worry about me to this degree.

"Which bridge is that?" I drunkenly pointed.

"Williamsburg bridge."

I stopped walking and stood in front of Jason. "Would your mother tell your father if she knew that you tried to kill yourself?"

"Yeah," Jason paused carefully. "Why?"

"You know last year? When I was hospitalized? My mom didn't tell my dad," I slurred my words.

"How do you know that?"

I looked down at my phone. Two missed calls from my father.

"I just do," I said, my voice small.

I thought my mother must have told my told my father, although I didn't even have the courage to tell her myself. A close friend had called 911, and I expected her to at least be worried. Instead, she ignored the issue and occasionally belittled me about my "little breakdown." I thought my father would have the same reaction, but wandering around the cobbled streets of New York, I understood that he wouldn't.

"She cares about you," Jason offered.

I struggled to believe Jason's sentiment, but I thought back to being that fourteen-year-old girl in my mother's class. I don't know if her project was directed at me, but it felt like it was. Maybe that was her way of caring. She didn't care in the sort of way one would want their mother to, but she did nonetheless. I never stopped thinking about what she had said: "If I had a gay child, I'd kill it."

My phone buzzed. Another text from my father.

"Jason," I asked, "can please we call a car?"

"Of course," he nodded.

***

A year later, my father and I are leaving a movie theater in Dallas. Although early Summer, the air felt unusually crisp and a breeze tangled my wavy red hair. I pushed my hair out of my face and prepared myself for my father's comments about the film we had just watched—a biopic about a gay singer from the seventies. It's dark when we left the theater and the skyline twinkled on the horizon. I smiled to myself when I noticed the LEDs on the buildings were glowing like a rainbow for Pride. Something about the city being lit up with all of the colors made my heart full.

"It was a pretty good movie," my father concluded. "I just don't see why they had to include the part about the man he was seeing."

"It would be dishonest if they didn't," I said.

"Yeah, but people knew he was gay. As soon as I saw him on stage, I thought well there's a queen. Why is there a need to show us?"

"Straight movies do that all the time."

"You're right, but there's no need to make a point of it," he said.

I stopped listening and watched the cars pass us on the freeway. By now, my father had to know I was a lesbian. Months ago, someone I had considered a friend attempted to out me to my family, and I worked hard to cover-up what had been said. I told my mother it was a lie, and she believed me, because she wanted to. With my father, however, I had told him about how I was no longer friends with this person because they had repeatedly called me homophobic slurs. This angered him, but he didn't acknowledge that I was targeted because I was queer.

He had to know, but there was no need to make a point of it. I anxiously chewed on a hangnail—wondering why some things were meant to be left unsaid.

***

I tiptoed back into the Midtown hotel around three thirty. My father was sitting at the couch, his reading glasses perched on his nose, while he read off his laptop. He immediately looked up as soon as he heard me open the door.

"Why didn't you answer my calls?" my father asked. I could tell he was upset with me because his Texas accent sounded thicker.

"I texted you. Jason walked me home." I said, stumbling as I tried to remove my boots. "You could have gone to sleep."

"I was worried," he said, slightly closing the lid to his laptop.

"I'm sorry," I offered, my heart heavy.

My father stood up and turned off the lamp, "it's okay."

Of All Things by Kate Ericksen

[Image Description: A digital drawing of a pair of transparent gender neutral figures kissing over a solid black background. They are embraced by a circular green alligator, biting its own tail. One figure has a red halo. The other figure has a red magnolia branch tucked behind their ear, and they are reaching out their hand with a rosary. This figure is wearing a grey, Bible-era robe with two interlocked red and white venus symbols on it. The yellow eye of the alligator lines up where the venus symbols interlock. The text "of all things visible and invisible" is in the top right above the figures. The drawing is bordered by a red and white line with a red and white icon in each corner. The top left icon is an eye. The top right icon is a cross. The bottom left icon is interlocking venus symbols. The bottom right icon is a tooth.]

Womb to Womb

Your womb to my unwanted womb.

I have your eyes, but we see things differently.

My DNA, copies of yours.

Yet you forced everything that makes me who I am behind closed doors.

Coercing womanhood became my chore.

Your love in exchange for obedience.

Imagine teaching your child that love would be the currency for their allowance.

You starved on denial, I wanted to feed you the truth.

I wore skirts to those revivals.

I went to your churches, and I sat in your pews.

I heard lies spewed and bigotry chewed in the mouths of men claiming it was the bread of life.

My knees and tears fell on altars.

I often asked god why you didn't just kill me by those halters like you promised?

Years later my throat can still feel the impression of your thumb

When you said you'd rather have a dead daughter than a queer one.

I repressed that memory for as long as I could, but not even opioids could make me numb enough.

Your body brought me into this world

Your hatred nearly took me out.

Imagine uprooting your own garden because you're that fearful of how it might sprout.

You bore two damnations, but I have never known something so divine as the spines of two children carrying an entire family's disapproval without burying themselves alive with the guilt you shoveled onto their immature graves.

Mom, to your god I prayed for change.

I prayed for peace.

I prayed for you.

I prayed for me.

There is not a world where I should have to be this proud to make it to my twenties. Where waking up is an achievement, and the epitome of resilience is me simply standing here breathing.

I slept on pillows of fear.

You made my bed out of shame.

I learned at age 13 some monsters don't hide,

They are in the next room, and they share your last name.

- Sterling Bentley

I'm Afraid of Snow

I am afraid of snow.

It covers me in drifts. Much like my parents Southern Baptist roots.
Blacks out the sky like the cigarettes I started smoking.
And chills me to the bone because I know…

In thirty-nine days.
I won't be seeing them again.
Until Christmas,

When God's child of forgiveness
Lets them forgive me.

- Kenna Lindsay

Untitled

The trauma I have endured
Because I am a woman
Because I am queer
Because I am no longer a Christian
In the South
Has been pervasive and unrelenting
Tied up in scripture and bless your hearts.

- Darci McFarland

Forgiveness by Sally Burnett

[Image Description: A white background with a collage of light sandstone rocks on the mid to lower part of the image with a large cross protruding from the center of the rocks. The cross is formed from a collage of gold glittery pieces filled in with yellow-gold marker with a pleated gold piece at the bottom, reminiscent of the tip of a mermaid tail. Across the horizontal portion of the cross, it reads: "Father, forgive them; for they know not what they do" twice; in the first line, "for they know not what they do" is upside down; in the second line, "Father, forgive them is upside down. The top portion of the vertical part of the cross reads "Father, forgive them; / for they know not / what they do" (line breaks indicated by the "/"). The bottom portion of the vertical part has the repeated sentence three times vertically, positioned similarly as the horizontal portion with parts of the sentence alternatingly upside down. The middle line is slightly longer, as it has an additional part repeated: "Father forgive them for they know." In the bottom right hand corner, there are smaller chunks of the sentence cut out and remixed, reading: "Father, / they know / forgive them; they know / Father, forgive them; forgive them for they know Father, / Father, forgive not Father forgive not for / what they do. Father, forgive not what they do. / forgive them; them; for they forgive not what they do. / they know what they do. they do / what they know Father, / forgive me / forgive."]

These Mountains Run Deep
By Lucy Parks

When I was a kid I used to walk out alone in the woods at night. When I started to get scared, I would breathe in the trees. At first their shadows would seem menacing, but I would connect with them and know that they were there to protect me, not to hurt me. When I did that, I knew that I would be safe. From the moment I learned to let the trees protect me, I felt like nothing in the woods would ever hurt me. For most of my childhood the woods became my safe place where I always felt happy and at peace.

My childhood on the mountain could almost be seen as idyllic. Our family never had lots of money, but we always had what we needed. The four of us ate a home-cooked dinner together every night and went for a walk in the woods afterwards, sometimes going down to the field by the creek for a family game of soccer. I had free run of our property, and although my parents didn't know it I gave myself free run of the neighbors' properties as well. I loved nothing more than being out in the woods, and by the time I was ten I knew every inch of forest within two miles. Our family was eccentric but tightly-knit, and Rooster Ridge became our own little universe.

My father and all of our family friends were musicians, and we spent a lot of time with other musicians and their families listening to them play. Their main genre was traditional Appalachian folk music, with plenty of other styles thrown in for good measure. My mom wasn't a musician (although she is now), but she was a storyteller who often got booked to tell folktales while my dad played music. When he wasn't playing music, my dad built instruments for a living - at least until money got too tight and he had to get a job at a nearby cabinet shop. As a kid I learned how to play a few instruments as well as some rudimentary woodworking skills, and I loved everything about all of it.

When I was nine years old, my father had cancer for the first time. He recovered, then was diagnosed and recovered again. When I was thirteen he was diagnosed a third time, and when I was 14, he died in the same hospital that I was born in. After Dad died, my mother moved my sister and I to a house in a nearby town. I was heartbroken. Dad and I had always shared a special kinship with our love of music, woodworking, and being outdoors. Not only had I lost my father who I loved dearly, I also lost our home on Rooster Ridge, the place that had defined my entire childhood and reminded me of him more than anything.

Not long after Dad died I started realizing that I was queer. I had always dressed like a boy and enjoyed "boy things," and I even played in a boy's soccer league and asked my parents repeatedly if I could join the Boy Scouts. I'd gotten made fun of surprisingly little through elementary school, but when I was still wearing boxer briefs in middle school the other kids started to notice that I was different and let me know that it was wrong. In high school I had been trying to dress a feminine as possible to avoid the name-calling and the stares, and I was determined to prove that I was normal and heterosexual like everyone else.

My parents were very accepting and even had gay friends, but I didn't really know what queerness was until I was probably 11 or 12. It was never a topic that we discussed. When we watched RENT at family movie night, I finally discovered exactly what queerness was. It wasn't just that I was a little strange - there was a whole new and exciting world out there of people who were deviant just like me. That new world excited me because it made me feel less lonesome, but it also scared me because it seemed like something that only existed in cities like New York. I didn't want to admit it at the time, but I knew that I was part of it. I just didn't want to be - especially when it felt so far away. So I tucked it in the back of my mind for a few years until I could no longer deny the feelings that I had.

I was lucky compared to most LGBTQ people where I grew up. My family was fairly progressive, and they had never taught me to be fearful or hateful. But we lived in a conservative, religious area, and I grew up hearing from friends, friends' parents, religious figures, and local media about how bad queerness was. When I started coming out to myself, I kept telling myself that my deep sadness and denial wasn't that I had an issue with queerness - it was just that I wanted it to be someone else's problem. I had been bullied so many times for my masculine appearance that I wanted to be straight just to prove everyone wrong about me. But it was me, and eventually I learned to embrace it.

The summer before I left for college I came out of the closet after a year or two of trying to hide it. I had been out to my close friends for a few months, but I had been captain of the women's soccer team, which was so religious that we (illegally) said a prayer before every game. I didn't want the other girls to feel like I was looking at them in the locker room or try to take me to church and save my soul, which enough people had already tried to do without even knowing I was gay. I finally came out publicly a few minutes after my high school graduation by shaving my head right in front of the school. After that I just assumed that everyone in town knew and stopped acting as if it was any kind of secret.

Once I realized I was queer, I felt like I was in a place where I had no future. I was alone. It didn't feel like there were any opportunities for dating, for love, or even just for not being the only person in the room who looked like me. I'd heard so much hate spewed towards LGBTQ people that I felt I couldn't go anywhere without having to look over my shoulder or at best getting sideways glances.

Although I've always been attached to the woods, it felt like I'd already lost them when we moved into town. And once I cut my hair short and started dressing how I truly felt comfortable, I got nervous being in the woods by myself. A lot of people out there have guns, and I was worried someone was going to have an issue with me in the wrong place at the wrong time. When it came to choosing the community I already had and moving somewhere that I wasn't always the odd one out, the choice was simple.

Moving to New York from rural Virginia was an experience like no other. At first all of the buildings and sounds and lights scared me. I got lost constantly. I resorted to my old strategy for learning a new patch of woods and went on long walks by myself, being sure to note landmarks and what direction I came from so I could find my way back. Once in a fit of malaise I just got on the train and I rode for hours, getting off to switch to a different train whenever it felt right. Eventually I learned my way around, and now I know the streets and subways better than many of my friends who grew up here. I've gotten used to the number of people, and also discovered that living in Brooklyn or Queens is much less stressful than Manhattan.

In this city I've always felt the need to explain myself and where I come from. People are shocked when they find out about our woodstove and lack of TV during my childhood, especially when I tell them that I was perfectly happy with the way things were. But often when I try to tell somebody about any of it, they just give me a blank look, like they're trying to understand but have no frame of reference to create a picture. Sometimes I'll make jokes about it just to get some type of reaction, but then when someone laughs at them I always feel a twinge of shame because they're laughing at me rather than with me. That, too, makes me feel lonely, like I'm from somewhere so foreign that it's impossible to even comprehend except as the butt of a joke.

After my first year in New York, I started to notice that when I went back home to visit it was getting harder to talk to people. Thick accents became a challenge for me. People didn't know much about New York past perhaps a family vacation to Times Square, and between being gay and living in the big city they just couldn't picture what my life must look like. Over the years, conversations about my life have waned and we stick to topics that everyone knows like small town drama, music, what everyone I went to school with is up to now. The longer I stay up in the city, the wider that gap gets, and the worse it makes me feel.

Many people in New York assume that I'm from a place so backwards that I must have no choice but to hate it. It's true that I had many negative experiences as an LGBTQ person there. But to be honest, I've also had lots of good experiences as an LGBTQ person there, and I've had plenty of bad ones in New York. I moved here so young and so shortly after coming out of the closet that it's sometimes difficult to sort out what's real and what's not because I simply don't have much comparison. There are definitely better laws in New York, but that doesn't always equal better treatment. Sometimes I wonder if it's really any worse back home than it is here, or if I've just been following a narrative I've been fed my whole life about how backwards rural areas are and how progressive and perfect cities are.

The duality between the big-city and the country versions of myself has led to an internal battle that's been raging for years. It feels like I can't be as safe, protected, and surrounded by beautiful queers if I'm living in Appalachia, but if I'm in New York, I'm missing the mountains and culture and all of the things that bring me back home. I've missed so many gatherings now that when I do show up people don't even recognize me. I've been unsuccessfully trying to find balance and wondering if there really is a way to be the proud queer nonbinary person that I am while still playing Appalachian Mountain Dulcimer in an old time jam. I'm not sure yet what the answer is, but I do know that New York isn't the place where I'll find out.

One of my first thoughts after the 2016 election was that I needed to move back to the mountains. I think that I can do some good there, probably more good than I can do here. There are strong pockets of resistance that are growing in Appalachia, and I think the place I will be most useful is building those pockets. It's much different to build resistance in the place that you're from than the place where you're a transplant, and it feels like it would be much more natural for me to do it at home.

Organizations like Queer Appalachia and the Stay Together Appalachian Youth (STAY) project, as well as online communities like Weird Appalachia, make me feel like maybe I wouldn't be so alone back there after all. Now I see conventions and gatherings posted online that I would love to attend if I was closer. Even seeing all of the queers posting on Personals from the rural South looking for love and friendship make me feel like I might be able to date and lead a life full of love there. They demonstrate that it's possible to be queer and Appalachian and maybe even happy and full of resistance. I think that I may not have seen it as a teenager, but there are other people who have felt the same way that I have and decided to stay and fight instead of running away.

When I came here, I thought that New York would always be my home. I was ready to leave everything behind me and start a new life for myself. I wanted to burn my whole life down and start something new. I'd been hanging on by a thread for a long time, and I saw escape as my only option.

But now, after six years here, I am discovering that there are a multitude of other options. My roots run much deeper than I ever thought they did. This city still doesn't feel like home, and I don't think that it ever will.

I'm ready to go back to the mountains and see what kind of life I can build there. I want a life where I can be as queer as I want to be and have love and fight for justice while drinking moonshine and playing old time on a Saturday night. I want to collect all the scattered pieces of me and try to fit them into one place, into one time. I'd like to believe that we live in a world where this is possible, and I am going to find out if I'm right.

What Am I Going To Tell My Mother?

What am I going to tell my mother?
About your tiny toes
Touching feet
Connecting to your thin thighs
That lead to love between your legs
I want to save from all the others.

Even though you don't need saving.

I love you.
how am I going to tell my mother?
that,
I love you.

The way your smile,
Spreads across your face

Lips like
Vegan butter
Spread
Across toast
Glosses with shimmering jam.

I want to
Break my fast with you.

To wake with your spine against my belly button
Your hair tickling my nose
Sea of cyan blue across cream and green.

How am I going to tell my mother?
That.

I long to lock lips with you
In our sapphic ocean
Warm waves of unconditional
Love lapping
Like tongues against your ear in the heat of this moment closing manifest destiny between your Thighs

How am I going to tell my mother?
That,
I am opposed to prop 8.[1]

- Kenna Lindsay

---

[1] Proposition 8, known informally as Prop 8, was a California ballot proposition and a state constitutional amendment passed in the November 2008 California state elections. The proposition was created by opponents of same-sex marriage in advance of the California Supreme Court's May 2008 appeal ruling, In re Marriage Cases, which followed the short-lived 2004 same-sex weddings controversy and found the previous ban on same-sex marriage (Proposition 22, 2000) unconstitutional. Proposition 8 was ruled unconstitutional by a federal court (on different grounds) in 2010, although the court decision did not go into effect until June 26, 2013, following the conclusion of proponents' appeals.

This is Me by Mary Beth Breshears

[Image description: This is Me is a self portrait of a woman on a white background slightly tilting her head upward with eyes closed. Her hair is constructed of embroidery designs that resemble geometric shapes and patterns in varying colors. The expression on the woman's face is a slight smile as if to say "This is me, authenticity, truly and unapologetically me."]

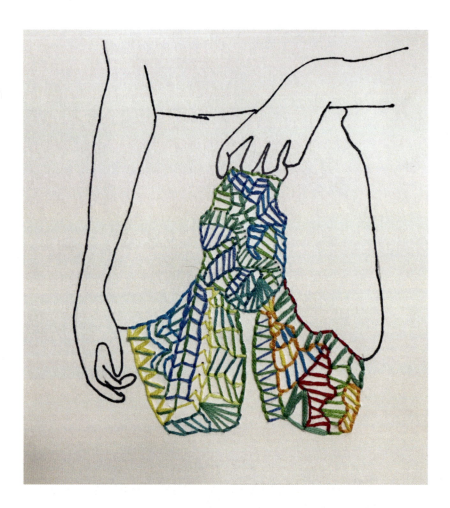

Show Me Yours by Mary Beth Breshears

[Image description: Show Me Yours is a portrait on a white background of the lower half of a female body donning a skirt, in which the figure is lifting to to show what's underneath. It reveals geometric patterns of various colors that cover the legs and groin. It's a play on the phrase "Show me yours, I'll show you mine."]

absolution

1. I fell asleep. In that time, the world caught on fire. None of that mattered. What mattered was her. She didn't wake me up. She just packed up our things and moved my sleeping body to the car. She saved us, without me even waking.

1. I uncork a bottle.
   Pour a glass.
   Take a sip.
   Every night the same.
   Different faces in the shelter,
   but the stories all start to sound the same.
   I sip and cut into my meat
   I eat my meal and cry in the bath.

1. What do you wish for?
   She asked it so simply,
   The wind blew through the chimes in her bedroom window
   and prisms danced on our naked, entangled skin
   Don't answer yet.
   There is time.

1. I hear my father's voice
   telling me to call gay people fairies
   asking if we can say the n-word now that there is a black president
   describing to me why he likes how that teenage girl looks.
   I hear him crying saying I abandoned him

And he doesn't understand why.

1. A woman came up to my father's car today
   Because she saw me crying.
   My father would not tell her why.
   Now he is crying.
   I walk her to her car.
   "I know why you were crying. That pastor is wrong. My sister is gay too."
   Why can she say that, a stranger, but not you?

1. Things I had learned by the age of six:
   Cookies are free at the grocery store
   Dogs will turn if you whistle
   The cat loves sticky fingers
   Grandma's teeth come out
   Falling down hurts
   Being tickled too hard can make you cry
   Leaves crunch under your feet
   Daddy is a liar.

1. "You should write that letter to him"
   "I know."
   "Don't put it off."
   "I know. I'm waiting till I'm ready."
   I say it, but I wonder will I ever be?
   Will I ever have enough money,
   ever feel stable enough,

have enough worth on

the table

to feel ready.

I don't send the letter.

-   Kat R. Vann

The Moon Beneath Her Feet by Donald Neel

[Image Description: A highly-textured dark blue background features a full moon with a rainbow halo illuminating a cold winter night scene. Shades of blue, black, and white, with hints of emerald green. The background also features a translucent film-negative style image of barren white trees. A translucent medieval-style image of the Virgin Mary stands in the foreground, eyes downcast, with a halo around her head.]

Sheep

do you speak with a bitter tang?
does your hatred taste sweet?

you gave away your criticism.
whose hands do yours belong to?

have you bargained your conscience?
replaced it with denial?

no will of your own making.
frantic, frantic, frantic to follow.

do you know what is righteous?
what you know is how i will burn.

do i deserve my flesh melted
in the fires of my misjudgment?

or is my burning a comfort
because you hold the match?

use my blood as lantern oil
to light your way.

cast your stones
until i crave the flames.

but hear this-

my way is my own.
i carve paths, roads, valleys.

i am not led.
i need not be.

i eat my own fruit.
i savor the sweetness.

no dog of yours can nip my heels.
i will not be swayed, be herded.

the lord may be your shepherd
but i am no sheep.

- Marion Rose Young

Thibodaux Pink Sky

Thibodaux pink sky,
as sweet as pumpkin pie.
Another kid born out of poverty,
another kin sent to the oil rigs to die.

For the green, for the green,
we haven't seen green in ages, our poles and trailers molded,
with formaldehyde, rust and other.. carcinogens.
That's the only green Evangeline will ever see.

When puffs of smoke come out of the DOW--
they say the sky is painted pink with chemicals.
My older sister is the one sent to clean the mess.
Free of chemicals--they say.
Except they don't count the ones in her lungs--
the chemicals breathed in by the unborn she's carryin'

We didn't have no science textbooks, let alone a chance to learn,
About the puffs of smoke hovering in the sky--
Or about the pollution rotting our lungs,
livers,
and our hearts.

We said "ya'll" and took pride,
but we didn't mean all ya'll.
We only meant *some of ya'll.*
Our double wide trailer was not big enough,
not big enough to hold the hearts of those,
we deemed sinners.

I was a sinner.
I am a sinner.

When I was younger, when I was younger,
I used to run from bullies until my feet blistered.
Until my knees cracked, like the same crack pecans make,
when opened up--vulnerable flesh--
What*ever* is made of our southern flesh!

Proud to be Southern!
But yet, I keep running from it,
not queer enough,
not trans enough,
to fit in the "gay mecca of Northampton."

It's as if a pipeline runs through my veins.
Like a trans cyborg--even in the "gay mecca"
I'm sub-human.
Or worse--just another butch--
That some "radical leftist" at Smith slept with,
just a temporary stop on your latest exploration of sexuality.

I think about how afraid my mom must have felt,
forced to keep her baby with just half a nursing degree.
I think about how guilty my dad must feel,
to know he was the jock that used to smash
the skulls of kids like me in.

I wish, I hope, I wait…
for a better day, a gayer day.
Where we don't turn our backs,
on our brothers and sisters in the South.

My best friend, my best friend,
got sent to conversion therapy.
My best brother, countless best brothers,
struggle with depression.
And I'm wondering--

when we will start checking in on each other.

We think that maybe if we act like cis men, hide our emotions,
that maybe no one will notice we are bleeding.
That we are drowning, from the neck down,
in toxic masculinity.
When we fought so damn hard to be free.

I think about the marks on my head,
that bows used to leave--
When I was dragged to Easter Mass,
in my sunday dress.
I hate those bows.
I hated the way I was misgendered.
And I hated the way that even other LGBT people used to tell me--
I was too pretty to be a boy.

I was too pretty to be a boy.
Too skinny to be a boy,
Too chubby to be a boy,
Too short,
Too emotional,
Too sensitive.
That I wasn't all that masculine--
Masculine people don't, "start drama"--
Asked if I was sure I wasn't *just gay.*

That I liked shopping too much?

I think about that conversation--
That conversation I had with my dad
He said, "I thought you were a feminist---
I guess if you couldn't beat 'em, you, *you*
Thought you would join 'em?"

As if my gender--my life--could be summarized by some twisted notion
Of what it means to seek justice in this world.

As if my masculinity,
only existed at the detriment of the
Feminine.

Sometimes at night,
I think about what my ma-maw used to teach me,
about good men,
She would tell me "Brooke-Ashley,
The only real way to get a good man's heart,
is through his stomach."

So I make sure to feed my wife's belly,
with home cooked meals every night.
to hold her every night,
as a homage and a *fuck you* to my
Southern Baptist roots.

Sometimes I take a deep breath,
to remind myself I can feel something
besides anger.

Sometimes I take a deep breath,
and all of the memories come rushing back.
"I don't think transmen have it bad,"
She says, she says "I don't think transmen
have it bad"

And I don't have it in me,
To tell her that every time I piss in public restrooms,
I hold my breath.
Hoping today, *today,* is not the day I get assaulted.

I think of what gravel roads used to feel like,
As we zipped down 'em on our four wheelers,
And about that time we flipped over,
dragged our bloody selves back to the cabin,
through cut sugar cane rows.

Sugar cane--
it's a fibrous, bitter paste,
when rubbed across wounds
that may never heal.

My step mom looked at me,
when she pulled me to the side,
and said, "Brooke, you were meant to leave this *fucking* place."
She said, "If you ever find yourself pregnant,
We are going to drive as far as we need to
and get rid of it."

"Don't tell your father."

Don't tell your father....
Years later, on my deathbed,
they never came.

They were not going to pull their son,
from the depths of depression,
to risk the grieving of their daughter.

Sometimes… sometimes, I grow plants
just to feel the dirt between my fingers,
To remind myself I come from dust,
And to dust I will return.

Sometimes, I think about the towers of sugar cane,
I used to pass on the way to my ma-maw's house.
She taught me how to catch fish,

skin em---
and deliver them to the men that paid for
our make-up.

I think about the shrimp--we used to buy by the pound
at Ralph's.
And the king cake she would make herself.
And wonder, when she was going to tell us,
her husband beat her.

That he took the bottle at night,
to wash down the days deeds at the rigs,
and took it out on his kids.

I think about how my dad used to cry when I got hurt,
but toxic masculinity beat that out of him too.

I think about how my ma-maw taught me,
how to tell a good watermelon,
from a bad one.
I wonder.. did she just get used to the bad ones?

- Elias Capello

elephant in your cupboard

and then you kissed her.
gazing into the cupboard of china teacups
rimmed in gold leaf with miniature blue birds
and blue elephants and blue bells
running around the rim
chasing ribbons of gold floating
in the soaked porcelain
white background
white like her cocktail dress
with crackly crinoline underneath.
the white dress, a round tea cup
the gold leaf, her hair in the street lamp.
the baby blue sash around her waist
was silk in your hands and when
you saw her reflection in the cabinet you
decided to kiss her.
you kissed her,
hands cupped,
as if clasped to a wine glass shaking in the
grasp of a frightened toast.
you kissed her
and the cupboard clattered, cracked in your wake
releasing a swell
        an ocean that
        breached over the both of you
        until you could not use the teacups

or saucers for floats
and you drowned.

- Kat R. Vann

bless the hushed mouths

the first time

the south

came to me

I made out

with her

on my bed

for hours

before her big brother

fetched her home

in time

for supper

because

her mama

said so

we tried to pretend

that she might could

that she was fixin' to

be like that

cousin of her's, Mary

living with her best friend

and that child they took in

in the mountains

near her Memaw's

but no one

wanted to

hear nothing
about it

we tried to gussy up
in Sunday best
to hide behind
a church smile
the one her dad
carried on
in front of his choir
til' it was worn
slap out
his mean it ugly
frown
greeting me
the yankee devil
with no shame
who tainted
Daddy's
girl

bless these
act like
you were
raised up right
parts
these have you
some more

chicken biscuit

cheddar grits

chocolate chess pie

in the fellowship hall

parts

these get you

a What-A-Burger

toothpick pickle on top

Cherry Lemon Sundrop

in a big ol' Styrofoam cup

with the good ice

at the #11

on Main Street

parts

bless the country

parts where

the mouths

of God-fearing

good women

cussed me

a hussy

bless the hushed mouths

of their granddaughters

who, even closeted,

were wide open

warm spaces

that first held

my cunt

and

my

heart

    -    Cristina Dominguez

Make a Joyful Noise Unto the Lord by Ayden Love

[Image Description: Sepia renderings of queers fucking, transposed on the pages of an old bible. The left page is cropped to show one figure sitting on the face of another. The right page is cropped to show one figures head between the legs of a reclined figure, offering Holy Devotions.]

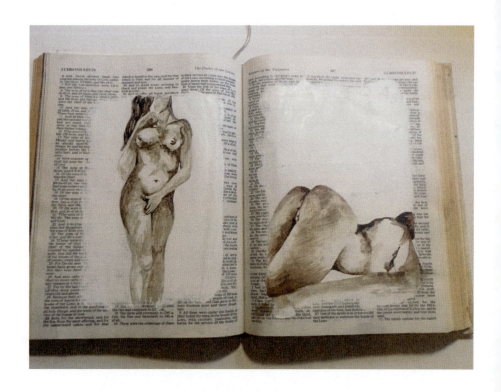

Lift Up Your Heart Unto the Lord by Ayden Love

[Image Description: Sepia paintings of human figures on the pages of an old bible. The left page shows a standing nude figure. The right page shows a figure from behind, on their stomach with their ass in the air.]

HOLY, gospel by Ayden Love

[Image Description: Black and white paintings of human figures on the pages of an old bible. Fragments of verses are highlighted in the background. The left page is closely cropped above a smirking mouth, wearing a collar and holding a vibrator necklace. The right page is closely cropped to show a bare chest, taken from a selfie angle.]

Glory to God in the Highest by Ayden Love

[Image Description: A painting that spans both pages of an old bible, of two figures entwined. One figure is semi reclined, while the other is draped across their stomach with their head between the others legs. Fragments of verses are highlighted in the background.]

Human

Earth, Warm, Life Sustaining, Comforting...
Heavy, Dark, Cold, Smothering, Screams muffled, cries Subdued.
Trying to fight, To claw my way out, But only more Earth.
Collapsing, hiding myself.
Like a bright flower hides its poison.
Afraid, Scared, Petrified of someone finding out.
Drowning in...

Water, Cool, Refreshing, Life Giving. Life Taking.
Warm, Salty, Running down my face.
Can't Stop.
Don't show them.
They won't understand.
They'll HATE you.
Try to swim, Keep your head above water.
Just keep Kicking, They must never know.
How it feels to pray, and pray asking GOD, anyone, to take it away.
To take you away.
Just keep Praying.
You're not trying hard enough.
People are starting to notice. LIE.
They must never know, Know that you tried.
But you're tired.
Tired of kicking, Tired of Praying.
Let go, Let yourself sink deep down into...

Fire, Heat, Warmth, Energy.

Eternal Damnation, Lost souls.

Liars, Adulterers, Murderers, Thieves.

What did I do?

Was I really that bad? I tried!

I really did.

I dated boys, went to church, did my schoolwork.

I kept my head down like a good girl.

But I couldn't change.

No matter how hard I tried, I couldn't.

PLEASE!

I don't belong here, I have to get out!

I have to get out!

Close my eyes and take a deep breath of...

Air! Gentle, Life Giving, Life Needing.

Open my eyes. It's over. The bad dream is over.

No hatred.

No hell.

No judge.

Just me, I can breathe, I can scream, shout, SING!

I am free, I am me, I AM

HUMAN.

- Elizabeth Lawrence

Staying Safe

Kiss your partner before you open the door.
Make sure the blinds are closed.
Once you step into the harsh outside world,
don't show affection and don't look back.

Walk.
Fast.
With your keys poised between your fingers,
like your life depends on it.

When you get home,
lock the door.
Check out the window for moving figures. Double check the lock.
Suffer through the heat at night because it's safer than opening the balcony door.

…

Check your pronouns before you open the door.
Make sure your clothes are cis.
Once you step into that office suite,
don't lower your voice and don't reveal yourself.

Work.
Hard.
With your body on display for all to verify,
like your livelihood depends on it.

When you get home,
lock the door.
Check out the window for moving figures.
Triple check the lock.
Suffer through the heat of day
because it's safer than
revealing yourself.

...

Take off your binder before you get to the door.
Make sure you look like the girl they raised.
Once you step into that house,
don't even think about coming out.

Laugh.
Loud.
With soprano voice singing femininity,
like your stability depends on it.

When you get home,
lock the door.
Check out the window for moving figures.
Quadruple check the lock.

Suffer through the heat during visits
because it's safer than
coming out to your family.

...

Secure your Pride gear before you open the door.
Make sure it's tucked away on the way to the parade.
Once you step into the rainbow sea,
don't stop scanning the crowds for guns and familiar faces.

Stay Alert.
With your partner held tight in your arms
like your love depends on it.

When you get home,
lock the door.
Check out the window for moving figures.

Quintuple check the lock.

Suffer through the heat in the closet because it's safer than losing all you've ever known.

...

Put on your clothes before you open the door.
Make sure you're comfortable.
Once you step into the harsh outside world,
don't return the stares and don't react.

Live.
Normally.
With your head held high
like your sanity depends on it.

When you get home,
ignore the lock on the door.
Don't check out the window -- there's probably moving figures.
Again, ignore the lock.
They would just find another way in.

Get used to the suffering heat
because it'll become your home
amidst the fires you'll walk through.

Your body doesn't get safety
in this world.

- Jordan Venditelli

Queer little wonders

on the same sunday that he slaughtered innocent,

i fell in love with a singer,

her voice swam around me, and i let myself forget

that in this life, we are not guaranteed a next breath.

his desire to kill was valued more than his victims' desire for loving comfort.

queer little wonders surround us, queer little loves, queer heartbeats

stopped mid song,

and maybe tomorrow a rainbow will signify that we reached dry ground

but for now we walk through blood,

our footprints showing where we've been, a map of past heartbeats.

- Flannery Quinn

Madam and Eve by Leanne Maxey

[Image Description: In "Madam and Eve," a Bible lays open on a vivid red couch cushion laced with a bright blue pattern. The book is held ajar by two rocks, and its white pages gleam bright cyan, yellow, and peachy orange along the seam. The larger rock resembles a heart, triangular with veins cutting across its center. On the right page is an illustration of two female figures strolling in a bright green forest.]

WHERE I COME FROM

I have relatives long gone, women
from the Old South who never married –
who lived in their aprons and their closets
and I think of that Mississippi

swelter, the suffocating silence
and so I say I have a girlfriend
and I say it on Thanksgiving
in the kitchen while my aunts

do the dishes and I think of my parents'
closed doors, the hushed words
behind them, how I never saw a kiss
or an *I love you* between them

and so I tell her I love how she touches
me, her gentle hands, the spell of her
kiss and I say I love her until I don't
feel so naked, or until even naked

feels safe and I say *that hurt*
my feelings even when it feels silly –
I fill the tension with words
until we scratch our way out

and I talk and I talk and I open
my mouth because they couldn't,
because they can't
Anymore.

        - Caroline Earleywine

Proverbs.

lavandula season in texas

leaves my legs itchy.

the height of grass and its infinite burrs run red races

up to my knees.

and my car, parked by the highway,

now counts more spiders than miles.

i am not complaining,

only noticing how this body and the world dance in unabashed collision.

purple petals fall across the dash,

and i wonder at the time between

each act of spontaneity:

today, i pull these supple stems with glee,

abandon final exams

and the medical bills.

last month, i closed my eyes

and kissed you through breathless panting.

tomorrow i will sit before the blank page

and hope for a miracle.

oh great goddess of the wide open spaces,

who tears us open into proverbial glory,

may the violet streaks of violence

never leave us too wounded

for the softness of sunday spring.

- emet ezell

I Gotta Ask

I heard someone say until all of us are free, then none of are

The freedom of expression of living I've never seen

Being a black sheep of my community

I wonder would Dr. King even talk to me or shake my hand or even call me his sister

I hope he would but I'll never know that

All I know is I'm always halfway accepted or fully rejected because I'm not sexually attracted to men

I mean I'm just not so I get the "oh you just haven't had the right man yet" or the Leviticus speech over and over again

I get stared at, invasive questions along with fake smiles

Sometimes no smiles at all I just get a confused look and a shaking head of disappointment

You don't even know me

So I'm benched because I'm down with the rainbow coalition

Who are you to judge and really who are you to choose what I fight for

I stand for equal rights across the board not for the who's suffered more contest

This wheel of misfortune y'all love to play

Y'all the same ones quoting Martin and Malcolm and haven't heard a thing they said

The house is divided and our problems still remain

I'm not your enemy, we all look the same to the flashing lights

So what I watch RuPaul at night and my best friend is drag queen named Sheila who does Cardi B impersonations

I'm still a victim of racial persecution and discrimination

Freedom will always be stationary until we all take a stand

So can I join in or what

- Zion McThomas

The Growing Season

"Susannah, Esther, Ruth, can you come here?"
Four pairs of bare feet scurried onto my porch,
       the porch their uncle built for me
"My hair is falling out too fast. I need you
To shave it. Please?" The oldest stepped up first.
She took the razor giggling as she cried,
still young enough to find the project fun,
but old enough to know what it meant.

My hair, much older than the child cutting it,
dropped slowly onto my rose bushes,
       muting their pink with my white.

I could tell they were afraid to hurt me.
The delicate responsibility
quickly bored my daughters' daughters
      one by one
they left the porch and ran into the bean field,
somewhere that their imaginations could
protect them in a way I never could.

I stayed on the porch and watched them dance
in the golden hour of the evening
my blonde hair following them, floating in
      the summer air, and mimicking
    all the emerging fireflies.
  -   Kelly Ann Graff

Jesus Saves

I am so tired of writing the same poem

The one

where the gay boy struggles

The Christian God hates

the boy is kicked out

of his home at 14

How God says this is acceptable.

How I became that boy

They became those rednecks

Small town

Piggly Wiggly parking lot

4 pick up trucks

Cowboy hats

Flannel shirts

smell of burning rubber

gravel spun in my face

How they circled

7 times for 7 days

waited for walls to fall

attack body like Jericho

Chanting

Yelling

Screaming

Quoting black and white verses

from their white Jesus

"Burn in Hell, Faggot"

"Fruit"

"Sodomite"

If I survived

I promised to burn my birth certificate in eulogy

Find exits hidden on highways

Ride as far west as I could go.

Still believing God existed

But He had Alzheimer's and had forgotten I existed.

They always

seem to find me

The name tags

Ties

White shirts

You call them Mormons

Jehovah Witness

Baptist

Methodist

I call them trigger warnings

The youth minister

Stretching body across desk

Throwing more Bible verses than punches

More punches than Bible verses.

Christians

Should taste their words

before they spit them

Stop confusing a

War on church

With not getting their way

There is no Greek or Hebrew word for being gay

The word homosexual did not appear in the King James Bible until 1946.

The religious edit the Bible

like poets

to score points

gather crowds

get laid

Beat the life out of another 14 year old in a parking lot

I am not writing this poem alone

Every day there is another Piggly Wiggly

Barbed wire fence

Gas chamber

Mother turning her back

Verse transformed murder weapon

Bible Study converted crime scene

When will we get tired of this poem?

So before you knock on my door

to tell me Jesus saves

tell me how he can save me from you

- Caleb Matthews

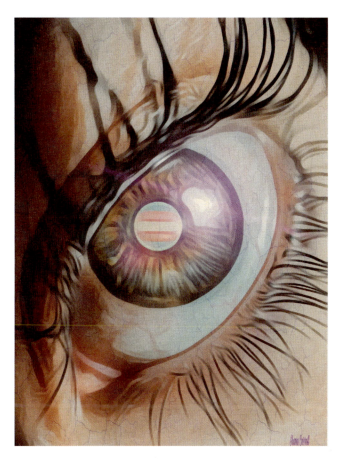

"Look Me in the Eyes" by Shoshanna Carroll

[Image Description: This image is of an oil painting that is full of simulated painted cracks and depicts a close up of a human eye. The person has a light skin tone and has long black eyelashes. The eye is full of colors that radiate out in lines of gold, brown, blues, and whites, with a painted light flare to the right of the pupil. Where the pupil would be is the trans flag with bars of light blue, light pink, white, light pink, and light blue. The painting calls on others to look trans people in the eye as they discuss us, our rights, and that they must truly see us, before they should say anything about us.]

When It Comes to My Parents, I'm a Secret Agent

Shoving gay porn magazines underneath a sunken mattress.
I turn everything over, locking it in night stands made of real oak.
Poems like this are written and read behind closed doors,
Barricaded with furniture.
The men moaning in gay porn videos
Are turned down to a whisper in case Mama walks by.
When I was fourteen, I almost got caught by my sister jacking off.
I have learned to lock doors since then.
If I feel someone walking throughout the house
In the middle of the night, the Play Boy channel becomes the *Food Network*.

When it comes to my parents, I'm under full investigation.
My phone conversations are bugged, there are hidden cameras
Throughout, in every corner, behind every mirror and figurine.
Mama waits up for me at three in the morning
In a built in porch, sitting in her rocking chair.
"Boy, where have you been?"
There's no sneaking in this house.
I can't get away with a damn thing.

- Shane Allison

Still Valid by Nour Hantouli

[Image Description: Colored pencil illustration in a warm color scheme featuring a neo-traditional tattoo-style, anthropomorphized deer's head and neck. The deer has eyelashes, fawn spots like freckles, and a playful smirk. On their hear is a prosthetic set of antlers on a headband. The portrait is bordered in at the bottom with a tattoo banner flanked by decorative leaves that says "Still Valid" in a neat script.]

Bent & Broken

I bent and broke

And bowed to the feet of a

god you said could never love me.

Just to see if he would try.

- Sterling Bentley

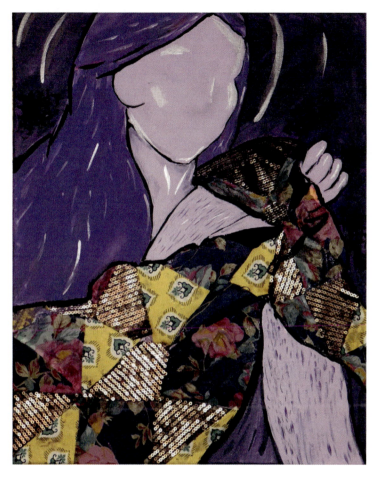

Quilted Queer by Amanda Balltrip

[Image Description: Quilted Queer is a 16x20 mixed media painting featuring a faceless feminine figure wrapping herself up in a quilt. The quilt is composed various fabric scraps including yellows, blues, pinks, floral designs, and gold sequins. A leg of the figure is sticking out, and it's hairy. The background, hair, and skin of the figure are various shades of purple, invoking a kind of royalty. The cheeks, nose, and forehead are highlighted with silver. Around the crown of the figure's head are also silver halo's. Perhaps she's shivering, or perhaps she's divine.]

Lavender

When I was a child I used to sneak into my neighbor's yard and eat the dandelions
 I'd creep in late at night, past the worn out gates and wild grass
And flower by flower, I'd wrap my lips upon those dandelions
I'd let their fluttering nectar drip down my chin
As their sweet scent coated my tongue in syrup
And I'd sit in the garden and swallow her flowers
Leaning back on my heels, my hands planted in the dirt
My fingers curling and clutching at clovers
I swallowed those dandelions one by one

As dawn slaughtered night, I blossomed along the buds
And once sweet petals fluttered down my throat and strangled me
As the friar foretold, violent delights with violent ends
My father ripped the petals from my lips and threw them to the wind
As his mother wept for my eternity in hell
I knelt in the pews while my pastor spat poison
And upon the flesh and blood, I was informed of my fate
Weeds, they said
Weeds, they preached
Dandelions were nothing but infections in gardens
A key to heaven tossed just out of reach

So I abandoned those weeds and planted new seeds
Seeds with an even thicker scent
And when they grew and spread upon my garden, the neighbors could sense it
Lavender
So from that day on I laced lavender upon my clothing
Entwined in my hair and stuck to my skin
Now instead of daintily dining on dandelions I devour lavender

Fist fulls of flowers, chewed and swallowed and some spat on my church grounds
Till my eyes roll back and my thighs turn purple

You piss me off until my fingers tremble
You call me angry when I snap
I suppose I'm stereotypical then
What, for standing and shouting upon schoolhouse desks
What, for storming from my chapel
Call me furious, I don't care
Call me a dyke, but I think you're just scared

Because you're aware deep down that you pushed me to this
You took my soft summer dandelions and crushed them beneath your feet
It's your turn
For you've tried my patience, though it was running dry
You've taken that sleeping beast and uprooted her
You've screamed in my face, hand clutched around your signs
Till I was forced to grow into a new type of flower
Oh, I'll show you mean, I'll show you brash
Look what you've made of me, breeder, I'm a Lavender Menace

- Hannah Elizabeth Seiler

A Woman Looking

A woman looking at men looking at women
A woman looking at women looking at men
A woman looking at hands
Folded in her lap
Gaze down
Avoiding
Shameful eyes of god

A woman looking at men looking at women
A woman looking at women looking at men
A woman looking at hair
Falling down the back of the pew ahead
ShinySilkySmooth
Flipping right at the ends into question made curly q

A woman looking at men looking at women
A woman looking at women looking at men
A woman looking around
Wondering if anyone is looking at her
Looking around
Seeing women
Wanting

A woman looking at men looking at women
A woman looking at women looking at men
A woman looking at asses
MenWomenAlike
Wondering what they would look like
Bent over
Backs arched
Cheeks flushed

Awomanlookingatmenlookingatwomenlookingatmenandlookingatwomen
Trying to convince herself once again:

Looks mean nothing
God isn't looking
Looking isn't touching
You can't be gay if you also look at men
A woman can't want women and men that's
sinfullewdperverted
All this looking
This coveting
This wanting
Awomanlookingatmenlookingatwomenlookingatmenandlookingatwomen
Looking to the heavens
Praying that looking isn't a sin
As long as it isn't acted on
Looking is just temptation
The devil worming their forked tongue
Into lusty folds
Lapping juices of a sinful woman's sinful being
Dirty talk into a mortal weaklings sinful ear
The devil has to be Woman if God is Man
Satan's the only reason this sinful woman
Could want anything other
Than a godly man

Why she is pulled into wanting women
Looking at women
Looking and wanting
More than to look like other women
But to bury her face
Into a soft shoulder
Same height
Soft flesh met under needy fingertips
Kneeling slowly
Making alto moans slowly escape moist pink lips
While speaking to less vocal lips
Equally moist
And pink…

But this is just the wanting
The sin lies in the doing

Back to the pew
She reaches for the hymn book
Hoping singing
Can drown out
The lust filled thoughts
And intense praying
Knees bent in the bedroom
Can keep these thoughts
This immorality
Merely tempting whispers of evil
And god's grace
A man's touch
Can make her good
Once again

- Peri Drury

Wet by Layla Padgett

[Image Description: This abstract painting resembling a vulva uses a beige skin tone color to create an oval shape, with many shades of pink ranging from light to almost red creating layers, leading to a deep blue slit in the middle. There are a couple of splashes of watercolor around and beneath the oval in pink and blue.]

rubyfruit --

my sweet pea
my sweet tea
my sweet peach

they cooed
they cried
they called

spreading what
to nourish
or to flourish
or to attract

yet it prickled
it soured

the cooing
and the crying
and the calling

for their nourishment

and the squalling
from a withering pea
and disintegrating peach
and sickening tea

straining to unearth
the sweetest pea

or the coolest tea
or the softest peach

that rubyfruit

- Lauren Beard

Return to Church

Sitting in a deep stained pew
Three rows
from the back
Hidden
Behind families
Little peeping eyes
Absorbing the message being spread
A woman speaks
Showing how progressive
A church can really be
"I love communion because every week I fall short and hope that by taking you, there is more of you and less of me."
Less of me
Less of me
Echoes in my head
Nice sentiment to doe eyed masses
It hurts
Remembering being asked
To be
Less of me
Less of me
Less of me
Less queer
Looking at girls
The curve of ass turned into spine
Less outspoken
About the injustices spread
Senseless teachings
Logical fallacies laced in the book
Less feminine
Because the femme is fatal
To the masc
A temptation of evil
As if I asked for you to be taught to look at me like that

Less ill and unstable
Head spinning out like a gear unchained
Fearfully hiding
Inside my room
Inside my head
Behind my hair
Wanting you to want me, need me, like me
Less curious
About the world
Things outside this small hamlet
About how we came into this eternal/transient being
Less accepting of doubt and dissent
That's the devil's work
Satan's whispers
In your susceptible womanly war
Less of me
More of you
Less of me
More of you
That's not how
To form a human
Autonomous
And self-actualized
But that's not what you want me to be
You want me to be a better version of you

- Peri Drury

Gran'mama Died Before I Was Gay by Hannah Cather

[Image Description: In the bottom two thirds of the page, oriented portrait style, is a six inch magnolia. In the top left corner, there is an aerial view of a pint of vanilla ice cream, cut in half. To the top right of the magnolia flower, there are seven two-inch pieces resembling feathers and coral. Around the magnolia, there are six lines of text in capital letters, which read: "as she stood / inside the baptist / church, looking through / a / window, a flock of birds / suddenly took flight." In the bottom left corner, there is a semi-circle and an image of clouds. The words "bloom and grow forever" are pasted on top. To the left of the words, in black pen handwriting, is "hc · 2019"]

Please Open Your Hymnals

Between you and me,

Even though I am mostly an adult, I have been searching for something,

Thoroughly searching for something my entire life, but I don't know what it is, not really,

How am I supposed to find something if I don't know what I'm looking for in the first place,

Oddly enough, I thought I found it multiple times, but to no avail,

Underneath all of the truth I have learned and discovered over the years,

My beliefs have not come to light, I don't know at all what I believe,

You see, what I was taught to believe is so full of holes and masks that I couldn't go back to that if I tried,

Very upsetting for my parents, but this is just the truth,

I often lie awake at night because I can't sleep, fears of a hell and accusations towards myself and my partner

Still have me with chills down my spine years later, how am I supposed to be spiritually healthy, embrace a religion or determine my own beliefs if

I'm always met with

Opposition, it's not my time to move on or to find the void I'm currently missing,

Not me, not yet, not today, but one day I will know, and maybe then I can sleep and my partner won't cry and my family will call me by my name, I will know.

- Kelsie Fitzpatrick

Thoughts and Prayers by Leeanne Maxey

[Image Description: The entire paper is drenched in a cool red. Thin crosshatched lines reveal the molding and shades of a window in the background. A tall plane rests against a roll of paper towels, its round, white top peeking out. On the plane are several felt shapes—a bright yellow star, a pink figure kneeling in front of a bush, two white doves flying toward her, and a rifle hovering above her head, pointed at the doves. In front of this scene lies a red leather book facedown, a cross zipper pull dangling in front of its splayed pages.]

Her vs Him

He thinks I'm sexy
He whispers it in my ear
A word he thinks romantic, I can hear it from the upward curves of his mouth.
All it really is is empty, an adjective that means nothing in the end
It makes me hollow - like a shell, a plastic doll he can fuck.

She says I'm everything and more.
In her, I radiate an infinite light
I reverberate into her spectrum - We intertwine to create something new
Something beautiful, an explosion of yellow, pink and blue
filtering to the strongest white.
I can't tell where I end from her.

He and I are distant even when he holds me close
like a coin down a never-ending well
The sound of him is almost nonexistent
An echo without a source
He is the flicker of a lightbulb attempting to stay bright

She is the electricity on the tips of a hand outstretched inches away from God
I am the match and she strikes ablaze,
holding me close - cupping her hands around me sheltering me as his wind wraps around.
Her beauty is in the notches of her spine and in the width of her shoulders
the same ones that carry her past strapped to her like a backpack.
It is the flicker in her irises when the sun hits just right - there to remind me that she's real.
It's in the warmth of her cheek when it rests sweetly in my palm.

She and I wrap together like the leather on a bible.
He is the pages in the index, barely clinging to the gold of the spine.

- Nyna Nickelson

Queer Foot First

You cannot possibly outrun

Your own footsteps

I have personally

Verified this

Fleeing the weaponized

Dogma they sold me

Praying away my very spirit

So rumored to be shameful

Escaping a God

They vowed would hate me

Shouting pleas for it to change me

Confused why it would not save me

Conceding into icy chasm

Where I became other

Other than you

Yet other than me too

Diminishing

In body

In voice

In spirit

Until love saved me

Warmth which survived

False prophecies

And broken promises

When Truth and Love

Rose me from all but dead

And I swore that I'd walk

Authentically this time

With sole still scarred from

Limping paths of danger

In cold condemnation

Through the jagged secrets

Carrying a soul some wished

Would shrivel and perish

So that none might follow those

Bloody tracks out of the closet

And in that blood I vow

For better and worse

My steps will always

Be queer foot first

    -    Haden Leevi

Cuntry Flag'n by (Gina) Mamone

[Image Description: This image is a digital collage composed of multiple hitachi magic wand shapes in various shades of green and black to resemble camouflage.]

How to Become
by Eryn Brothers

Part Firsts

It will begin on a playground. You are five or six, scraping the early nineties with your Aladdin sneakers, digging your hands in the small town dirt of the private school sandbox. There is a girl, her name is Beth, and desperately you cling to her pointy face and rigid ponytail for friendship. You have dug in the dirt with her before and wish to maintain this golden ideal. This, the importance of friendship, has been a sermon in the first years of your life. Your television told you that you should have friends. So did your mother and sister. Looking at Beth and her pinched face, never seeing your own pudgy one reflected in hers, you know that there is work in being this girl's friend. The other girls give each other plastic trinkets, full of fake strawberry smell and pink baubles, echoing their eerily adult laughter. You have dirt.

Though the adult vernacular will not grace your tongue, there is an understanding that you are "other" compared to your schoolmates. There is an intuitive knowledge of the language of objects - Beth's dress is new from JCPenny, your overalls were sewn and patched by your mother. Beth has two bags; one a plastic purse and a crisp purple backpack. You have a thrift store bag, with knock off brand Looney Toons staring aimlessly in dowdy abandon. This is the first Otherness.

How do you please Beth? You only have dirt and affection to give, stories to tell her that you make up about your dollar store barbies, songs to sing that you learned from the three tapes your mother owns. This satisfies her to an extent, and every recess is a happy one, your home haircut bobbing behind Beth's starched tutelage. At first, the games are fun. They are full of swings and fantasy, characters brought to life out of word and air. One day Beth comes to recess, sad eyed. Her Mother told her no more rough housing during recess (she tore her white tights the day before during a debacle with a monkey bar dragon), and so the games had to become docile. Easy. Demure.

This is hard for you. As much as you love your dirt, you also love Beth. Beth is your friend! She forsook every bubblegum whim to fight foes and charm villains in the span of thirty minutes every day. There were never words during class or school, but during recess and after school, the kingdom was ruled by two of you. When Beth implores to play soft and timid, you have no idea what to play. Your face will squish into a confused chipmunk perplexity and you will give Beth the wheel that she always had but never had enough imagination for.

"Let's play Beauty and the Beast. I'm Belle. You're the Beast."

From there, the game changes, and drastically at that. Beth tells you to throw out your chest when you are Gaston. You silly putty your face to be LeFou. Your shoulders hunch with the burden of a curse when you are The Beast. At home, you look at your face and body in the mirror for long stretches of time. Are you ugly? Are you mannish? If so, are you ugly because you are mannish or mannish because you are ugly?

It becomes too much. The wooden words and feelings of a child cannot communicate how you feel to Beth, so you start taking books to school. You read on the playground after school waiting for your mom. You are tired of being ugly. Beth does not see this as a slight, and for awhile she goes back to her bauble friends and pink world, and you are content getting lost with Rohld Dahl or Lewis Carrol. You find yourself in women who are inquisitive and adventurous, girls who exist only in the playgrounds of the brambles of the wild heart you are told to silence.

It makes you happy.

After weeks of this, Beth corners you at recess. "Wanna play?"

Maybe it was a particularly lonely day. In your mind's eye, it's a rainy fall afternoon, the mulch of the playground wafting its spicy, sickly earthy smell. You might have just finished your book, and the poetics of nuance are just a memorial metaphor to justify what happens. Regardless, you put your book away, and go to play with her. It's Beauty and the Beast again, but the story gets sped up to the end. Beth allows you to transform into the prince, a dramatic spectacle that draws a few looks from your peers. Impatient and tired of the audience, Beth, with crossed arms and pointed eyes, tells you that it's the end of the story. You start to shrug and suggest another game, but your Belle ushers you into the jungle gym. This jungle gym, true to wealthy schools, is stacked. A large, private crawling tube connects one piece of the castle to another, and this is where she leads you.

It's raining. You hear the sprinkle and spray of the coming storm. The teacher will call the flock in soon, and you start praying for the sky to break. Something about Beth's clipped direction makes you uncomfortable. She looks at you out of the side of your eyes, and sits with you in the tube. The cacophony of children can be heard commingling with the rain beating down on the plastic above your head, and Beth says, "Now Belle and the Beast have to kiss. That's how the story ends."

You do not hide your shock. Kissing does not bother you - you kiss your mother's powdery cigarette cheeks, you kiss your doll, Laura, before sleeping, you kiss dogs and cats and your sister, but the kind of kiss Beth is suggesting is an Adult Kiss, capital lettered and not something you desire in any way. You shake your head, sticky bangs clinging to your forehead. "No," cannot come from your mouth. Your voice comes with courage, and you say, "Won't we get in trouble?"

Beth purses her lips, slick with authority and a strange maturity that upon later, older reflection cause you to wonder about her home life. The compressed ultra femininity the girl expresses in her skirts and dresses, shiny mary jane shoes, curious primal knowledge is so far away from your own, and for the first time in your life (though not the last) you wonder if she is aware of something that you have not been privy to. "We won't get in trouble," Beth says, brushing your consent away, "Because no one can see us in here."

Seconds of worry, of the desire for acceptance, love, appreciation, and friendship course through your tiny body. "Ok. But not a long kiss. That's gross." You squint your eyes, driving the point home that kissing like an Adult is just not your style. Beth rolls her eyes, and leans in.

You will go back to your books, allow your body to become chubby for fear of playing. These are the first steps to you being friendless for years and not caring. Of being Other.

You will be happy. I promise.

It's your first kiss, and it's wasted on a bitch who will never speak to you again.

Part Drag

You become obsessed with the occult at the ripe age of ten. You start demanding to wear black, which sort of frightens your father ("Black just isn't for kids, kiddo," he says, slurping a tequila after dinner) and delights your mother ("I think it's quite slimming, Chris," she says, slurping a cigarette with her after dinner coffee.) You delve into every book that deals with witches, vampires, werewolves, ghosts, anything that is the exact opposite of everything that you are told to like-barbies, boys, makeup, crushes, fairies, princesses. These things are soft, and you are tired of being soft. You are tired of being pushed around by teachers and bullies, the stories they create about you.

It is often disputed where the terminology of "queen," comes from or the original intent of its meaning. In Dutch, "kween" translates to "barren cow," or "woman past the age of baring" where as in Old Saxon "cwena" simply meant "woman," or "female serf." In Middle English, we find "quene" which suggests a ruddy, young woman, and in Old English we go back to "woman" or "wife."

King does not have the same interesting etymological history. A king has always been a king, a man with power. It is its own separate entity from manhood, and yet symbolizes the process so completely in many a cultural norm. What boy would not want to be king, if not even for a day? To rule with no questions asked? It seems as though queens were not so lucky.

Though this understanding of etymology is not yours at the age of ten, reading fairytales and fantasy novels at a disturbing rate, this concept is glaringly obvious. In most tales, the King represents the land and all of the doings in it. To earn this kingdom, one had to sacrifice and toil, to be heroic. Yet you find yourself angry at the women, from barren cows to queens, who are idle in these yarns. You want them to display the heroic effort that you feel simply by just existing. You want them to crawl the mountains you are afraid of, scale treacherous destinies that you feel so out of your grasp growing up fat and lonely in Arkansas.

Some of them did. Alice, Matilda, Hermione, Cimorene. These young women galvanize you, forage your imagination and inventive spirit commonly looked down upon by your peers. You are not as wild as your little sister, who at the age of three does not give A Flying Fuck about a God Damn Thing and scurries the back yard naked as a blue jay, eating mulberries off the ground (you only primly pick them off the tree.) Your kid sister pisses on the ground, and sympathy cries with you when the kids are assholes to you at school. She is wild. You are soft, in your body and heart, and it makes you an easy target, just like those barren cows and queens, princesses, and destined women.

So you decide to remove anything garishly and conceivably feminine from your life. Anything that you are told is "girly," you sneer at. You become obsessed with music and learn everything about it, every dumbass fact about every dumbass album you find yourself falling in love with. This is a strange symptom of your anti-girl campaign, especially during a time period where girl power and riot girl is rampant. When your older sister starts asking for make up and perfume, you roll your eyes and sigh. You want to get away from anything soft, sensitive, light, pink, or endearing. You want gristle, guts, shadow, bristle, fang, and tooth.

In retrospect, these are the first steps to you being a closet goth and sad bastard for life. A more adult Otherness, albeit self imposed.

During this time of voracious hunting for the Grossest and Most Disturbing Things You Can Get Your Hands On, you stumble across The Phantom of the Opera. Whatever rendition it was in, Chaney or Webber, take your pick, the story touches you. At this point, you have convinced yourself that you are The Most Unlovable Person in Creation, and that if someone, anyone gave you a Chance that you would be able to show the world that looks and weirdness were not everything. The Phantom spoke to you. A monster, hiding in plain sight, holding great talent that was something closer to beauty than looks. Upon reading this tale as an adult, you will understand how grossly you misunderstood the allegory.

Like any child at this age, you decide to take this poignant ideology and transmogrify it in the only way you know how. Halloween.

You beg your mother to allow you to be the Phantom for Halloween. It is a long campaign, full of tears and fury, but finally, she allows you to buy a cheap K-Mart half mask, gooey green monster makeup, and a cape. When you don the trifecta of the costume over a black turtleneck, faded grey jeans, and knock off converse shoes, something about the facade feels incorrect, astray.

Your long hair whispers next to your tits that will bust out in the coming year. It confuses the costume, the strange mix of princess long hair and what you want to be for the night. You squint, the makeup cracking on your face. How do you abolish this nuance for the evening?

Decidedly, you pull your hair into a ponytail, parting it to the side. You tuck it into the back of the turtleneck, and using your mother's Aqua Net, slick the sides back. Your eyebrows are already thick with puberty approaching, and there are strange downy sideburns where your hair wants to grow but cannot. You smile. You are complete.

That evening, you waltz into your elementary school's Halloween Carnival. Parents do not try to conceal their dislike for your new persona, the other children are too cranked up on the sweet potion of socializing and candy to care. You strut about the halls, fluorescent and poorly decorated, the polyester spiderwebs jumping out like a bad prank next to subtly Christian decor. Paper pumpkins smile at you, teachers hand you candy, bored. A couple of cast iron blonde mothers ask you what you are supposed to be in their feigned polite southern manner, but the mask protects you. It allows you the privilege of being rude. You just brush your hand in a flippant manner, and turn your heel to the next game. It's liberating, the luxury of silence. Usually your hair is patted, your cheeks pinched, people ask if you have a boyfriend or what your favorite toy is. Small talk is exhausting, but even more so when you are a girl child. Always the same questions, always the same expectations in answers.

You deposit your candy with your parents, who will likely get stoned later at home and eat all of your Snickers bars. You turn the hallways to the bathroom, march into the girl's room. Before entering, a little boy, maybe three or four years old, toddling with his mother, sees you, gasps, and points.

"Mom! Why is that boy going to the girl's bafoom?"

You don't wait to hear the mother's answer, though you cannot imagine that it was too kind. A smile grows from your chest, underneath your Future Tits, from deep in the caverns of your wildest heart. It leaps up your throat, jumps to your eyes and mouth, and as you step into the stall, you look in the mirror. You take off the mask and laugh. Your work is done. You are convincing. You fooled them. You are more than masks, you are more than Aqua Net. You are more than long brown hair that your mother refuses to cut short. You are more than the black clothes, you are more than small talk.

You, my dear, you are a king.

Part Feed

the first time your made yourself throw up it was
because your mother gave you a trashy YA novel about eating disorders
and because you don't know how to be a girl
and because you don't know how to be thin
she thinks that you're gonna get an eating disorder
or secretly hopes you will soon.
Something about bones
makes your mother know
that you will be beautiful
and if you are beautiful
you can be anything.
Your sisters

in dresses
are told that they are pretty
your older sister says
make up won't fix ugly
and laughs at you.
Your mother looks at your chucks and shitty hair
and says
"Start wearing low cut things, the boys will like you,"
you are twelve.
At fourteen you are staring at the toilet
you know you are fat
and that you like girls
and boys
and guitars
and books
and records
and comics
and quoting monty python with your best friend
and you know that arkansas is too small for you
because sometimes it is ok to be big
but for right now - you gotta make yourself small.

You don't wear low cut shirts
but you kissed Sam at a party
and her freckles and your freckles kissed too
and that feels better than being thin you think.
but Sam has boys and girls who like her
and doesn't want anyone to know.
If mom only knew.
She thinks dykes are ugly
mannish masculine and impotent
you blast REBEL GIRL at full volume
so she is forced to hear DYKE
in her home over and over.
At the toilet you are fourteen
and Sam and Danny are dating

and they both kissed you at some point
but you weren't thin enough
that's what Danny told you
if you were pretty Sam wouldn't need to lie.
your stomach pops gently over your jeans after dinner
and you say my god one day
i will be so big
i will be all the things i love
i will be beautiful
but right now you gotta make yourself small.
so you point your finger and try to press
that magic button that says THIN
and the stupid YA book made it seem so easy
and your mom made it so easy to look down and go
bigger is not better
and when you think one finger won't do
you put in two
like how all the men you let touch you later will do to your other mouth
aggressive and weak all at once, fumbling to make something happen
and this
is how you make yourself small
for the first time.

Part Identity

I wish there was a pronoun that explained that I love metal but cry every time I watch Funny Girl.

I wish there was a pronoun that said I wrote my first song when I was eleven years old and no one has ever heard it except for me.

I wish there was a pronoun for how sorry I am for how cruel to other women I have been.

I wish there was a pronoun for how careless I have been with men.

I wish there was a pronoun for the fact that I have never hated my freckles or the strange birthmarks that pepper my body.

I wish there was a pronoun for how I want to make my parents proud.

I wish there was a pronoun that proclaimed my love of lipstick but my hatred of heels, that I covet dresses but always buy jeans.

I wish there was a pronoun for how much I miss my grandparents.

I wish there was a pronoun for the fact that I volunteer my time to my community and deeply look up to those who dedicate their lives and careers to making the world a better place.

I wish there was a pronoun for how complete I feel when I spend time alone.

I wish there was a pronoun for how grateful I am for my friends.

I wish there was a pronoun for how lucky I have been through my personal growth - that I have been tethered with love, support, and places to weather the storm.

I wish there was a pronoun for the family I do not know but have suffered and fought for me.

I wish there was a pronoun for the family that continues to fight still.

I wish there was a pronoun for how proud I can feel for myself after finishing a song, a poem, a piece of work, a bike ride, or a drawing.

I wish there was a pronoun for my ability to cook, for how much I love gathering people around a table to become a makeshift home.

I wish there was a pronoun that would explain how much I love my body now, after the years of abusing it with drugs, alcohol, eating disorders, bad love, dangerous sex, and mental swords.

I wish there was a pronoun that made up for the lost time of not loving who I wanted to love, of not fucking who I wanted to fuck, of not caring for who I wanted to care for.

I wish there was a pronoun for the fact that I have learned a lot.

I wish there was a pronoun for the fact that I have a lot more to learn.

I wish there was a pronoun for the work in progress that I used to be ashamed of.

I wish there was a pronoun for the work I will die doing.

I wish there was a pronoun for how much of myself I have become.

On the last Sunday of September

It's nighttime

On the last Sunday of September

In the parking lot

Of the restaurant where

My girlfriend and I

Went to dinner

In a town you've never heard of

In Indian Country

In the Bible Belt

In the land of 100 churches.

We stand close

Talking and kissing

Embracing

Tit to tit

I lean in to kiss her

Once, and again

And laugh and talk

As the moonlight shines

On our brown faces

Illuminating

Our united lips

And woven bodies.

The restaurant closes

Customers, strangers

Migrate

From the restaurant

To their own cars

They walk around us

Ignored, but watching

I kiss her in front of strangers

And worry

She lives here

This is her city

These strangers are her neighbors

I am only visiting

Our kisses are rare

Sweet, enticing

I will miss her when I'm gone

So I steal another kiss.

She isn't worried

Even when another woman

Walks in between us

Instead of around

To get to this woman's car

Brusquely, rudely, violently

Yelling, "Excuse me!"

Forcing us apart.

After the woman passes

My girlfriend and I

We make faces

At each other

"I guess she's religious?"

I laugh, nervously

"She must be"

Shrugging off negative energy

Thrust upon us

By the crumbled steeples

Dotting the corners

Of every street

In this pious town.

This prairie land

Dotted with cowboy hats

And ancient oppression

Engulfs us

As we laugh and love

And say our goodbyes

On borrowed time.

    -    Fernande Galindo

The Open Relationship by Shannon Novak

[Image description: This work represents one of the sins I was judged for when I underwent conversion therapy - the open relationship. It is a large work on canvas that uses a mix of paint and ink to create a series of hard-edged isosceles triangles that swim in a cerulean sea of gestural brush strokes. The triangles represent the various parties (people) that participate in the open relationship; myself, my partner, and other men. They are irregularly spaced from each other, sometimes overlapping which reflects the varying degrees of emotional closeness between each person. The background represents the chaotic world that underpins the relationship - a swirling ocean of people, places, demands, and time.]

Eulogy for Gomer

Jim Nabors died today.
He played Gomer Pyle and was on Andy Griffith
And could sing, Lord could he ever.
He's one of 3 things my
Tiny, backward hometown is famous for.
My mother lived for a time just steps from his mother.
Everybody of a certain age had Jim stories.
My high school's centennial yearbook
Featured him proudly.

I always loved that someone so famous—
Went to my high school,
Grew up in my hometown.
He took off to California to make it big
Wikipedia says it was also for his asthma.

Bullshit—

When he and Stan married in 2013
They'd been together 38 years.
He didn't suddenly find gayness
Like a jailhouse Christian finds Jesus,
He left our hometown
Because he knew he'd die
A retiree from the mill with a plump well-kept wife
And 2.5 beautiful children—
Quarterbacks or Miss Alabamas
All quietly shading the closet door,
Standing so close together
You wouldn't see a sliver of rainbow between them.

The main highway back home
Is the Jim Nabors Highway
From down below the Hardee's,

My elementary school, and the quarry
To somewhere up past where Miz Hodges
Got thwacked by that meteorite
65 mph past the Texaco and the Wal-Mart
Will put you over Merkle Mountain
And pointed towards the closest airport.

I'd like to think the decision maker on that naming knew that
Crawling out of the blasted earth
Violence beaten purity plastered on your life like shiny marble tiles
65 mph past the one and only time God's slingshot hit home—
A freak occurrence but proof that their divine father
Would, in fact, aim if he takes a mind to—
To Birmingham—the big city—
Airport and gone
Was the only way people like us would survive,
So they planted the sign
Gave us a guidepost
Which we read by closet light
Planning escapes
Some more successful than others—
Some damn spectacular—
Some by way of the cemetery down past the old Super Foods,
The skating rink, and Thrill Hill.

He was front page news back home, of course—
Sylacauga native
Andy Griffith Show star
Jim Nabors has died.
They called Stan longtime partner and mention the wedding
Far more than I ever believed they would do.

    -    Dawn Betts-Green

A Tourist

When I was a child
I remember
Watching my friends change clothes
Through the corner of my eyes
In the mirror's reflection
Feeling guilty.

In fifth grade they called me 'gay.'
My mom told me that it meant happy,
But the way they said it
Made me feel like
Gay was a bad word.

I picked straight,
Because straight was easier
For the longest time.

Now, I'm treated like a tourist.
And my friends still tell me that I'm not *really* queer
That I don't belong here.

      - Zoie McNeill

The Choice by Leeanne Maxey

[Image Description: "The Choice" is a field of blue green grass, yellow highlights balancing on the edges of blades turned every possible direction. The composition is vertically split by a cluster of seven small white flowers on the left and a palm-sized grass-green Gideon New Testament on the right. The flowers, called bleeding hearts, are heart shaped but with wings and folded heads, like tiny serious chickens; the book is beneath a pile of smooth bluish grey and white stones, each individually pebbled or crisscrossed with minerals.]

"Penance"
by Emma Fredrick

Inspired by *Oranges are Not the Only Fruit* by Jeanette Winterson

I do not
repent.
Love is
not a
sin. And
God knows my love for her was more
holy than your prayers have ever
been. But I do my time, ice cream trucks
and dead bodies with so many flowers
bent into
crosses.
I wonder
if they
could
bear the
weight of
my love.

My Only Sin is Being A Woman by Briheda Haylock

[Image Description: This image is a black and white photo on a skewed angle of a half body shot of a young woman leaning on an unfinished, cement fence with a plantain tree behind her. Her curly hair covers her face as her head tilts downward focusing on the black rose held in her hand. As she rests on the wall wearing only her curves, black pearls that reaches just above her navel, and panties resting on her hip, she searches for hope.]

Bless Your Heart
By Heather Stout

When I jokingly tell people at work I come from humble hillbilly stock, it's no joke. My family has lived in the same Arkansas valley of the Ozark Mountains for over 200 years. The women I come from lived hardscrabble lives in the mountains surviving all sorts of things I can't imagine. Perhaps those deep roots are both why it took me so long to finally come out and why I had the strength to finally do it.

Coming to terms with who I am was a slow process. I think I always knew I was a dyke. I've been obsessed with women my entire life. I wanted to be beautiful and adored like Judy Garland and the other women of Old Hollywood. I wanted to be fierce and strong like Xena and her girlfriend Gabrielle. I spent time and effort fashioning myself into the lovechild of Dolly Parton and Elvira, two of the campiest women in history. I made constant jokes about how "it ain't real friendship if they don't say it's gay" about various female best friends. I even started a running list of "Female Celebrities I'd Turn For" when I was 13, assuring myself it was something every straight woman must surely do. For years I ignored what I knew to be true. I couldn't admit I was a lesbian. Not there, not at home, not in the South. I remembered the shit people said in high school about The Gays, the nebulous glob of dykes and faggots who existed to guide you off the path to Heaven straight into Hell.

Homophobia exists beyond the South, but it's definitely a more concentrated form in Conservative areas because of the stranglehold of religion. Anyone who grew up down South understands that, even if you aren't personally religious, religion Does Something To You whilst living there. Flannery O'Connor once said, "But approaching the subject from the standpoint of the writer, I think it is safe to say that while the South is hardly Christ-centered, it is most certainly Christ-haunted."[2] A professed love of Jesus is as ubiquitous down South as our beloved sweet tea. Hell, church denominations determine cliques in high school (at least

---

[2] Flannery O' Connor, "Some Aspects of the Grotesque in Southern Fiction", http://www.en.utexas.edu/Classes/Bremen/e316k/316kprivate/scans/grotesque.html

in mine). As a Southern Queer, you are constantly reminded that being gay is a sin. Your dirty attraction to someone like you is simply the Devil himself playing tricks on you! Who cares if repressing your natural desires makes you miserable? You are to follow God's word and if that means you suffer your entire Earthly life, so be it. You'll be repaid in Heaven! It is a message that is fed to you over and over and over. It took years for me to be able to admit to myself that my attraction to other women was not disgusting or some kind of sin.

The sheer fear of being called a dyke, a Godless sinner, was enough to make me stay in the closet until I was 21. In fact, I had to be on a whole other continent before I could admit I wasn't straight. I studied abroad at Oxford in 2011. It was magical. I was away from anything and everything I had ever known. I could finally let down every guard I had up and let myself live. I ended up falling for someone in England, someone who was a woman, which resulted into a mini mental breakdown. How could I possibly fall for a woman? I wrestled with my feelings privately for weeks and then, on what would have been Judy Garland's 89th birthday, I came out to a friend for the first time. I initially identified as bisexual-- not because that sexuality is a stepping stone, but because I was afraid to admit being attracted to men at all was just a manifestation of compulsory heterosexuality. The friend didn't take it well and filled me with shame. Ignoring their hurtful words, I decided to come out to my other friends in Oxford. Their support made me feel safe enough to come out to my beloved Hendrix College friends back in Arkansas. I came out on my college campus senior year and slowly came out to other friends. I was out to my immediate family, but still full of fear. I remember getting very drunk, flirting with women, and drunk-texting my older brother to ask if he thought our parents still loved me. I was so worried about my sinful life driving way the people I loved. But being open about who I was started changing things within me.

Eventually I stopped caring what people thought about me, deciding instead to just bless their hearts and move on. I stopped calling myself bisexual, realizing I was never actually attracted to men. I would talk about queer issues, but I never explicitly stated I was part of the LGBTQ community. Those who were close to me knew and that's all that mattered. But 5 years and 2 days after I came out, a man opened fire on my community in a safe space, killing 49 and injuring 53 at Pulse Nightclub on their Latinx night. Their deaths made me feel compelled to finally be Fully Out. I began saying "we" when discussing queer Southerners on Facebook. I changed my orientation online. I said aloud that I was a high femme lesbian and proud of it. But changing shit on social media doesn't mean you're finished. Coming out is a constant process that happens almost daily, on purpose or otherwise. I'll end up coming out to strangers if I mention the world "girlfriend" or (soon) "wife." I'm always hyper aware of people realizing my fiance and I are a couple when we go out. It's not hard to tell. I love holding her hand and putting my head on her shoulder. We're proud of who we are and of our love, but sometimes it just isn't safe. The Trump administration has emboldened those who hate my community. Lesbians are not more acceptable, we're just a really popular category of porn. The preexisting hate down South seems more apparent every single day.

The South will always be my home, even if it doesn't want me there. It took me YEARS to be happy and secure in my lesbianism. I wasn't really myself until I was fully out. Now I'm engaged to the most thoughtful woman in the world. I am happier now than I've ever been. This femme is never going back in the closet, y'all.

God's Plan

GOD is SO good!

if you forget, check the neighbors sign in their front yard

their house is being foreclosed because they can't afford to live

there anymore. I heard it was because their dad left and their mom tried

to commit suicide

GOD is SO good!

if you forget, walk down to the riverbank pick up a rock and look

at all of the creatures hiding underneath

pick out all of the plastic bits and throw them back into the river, they're hindering

your view of the beauty of nature

GOD is SO good!

this news story says gay people can get married now

this news story says another cop killed another black kid

this news story says gay people can kill gay people who weren't born here

this news story says trans women's average life expectancy is 35

this news story says a trans woman can kill a trans woman or a kid

for America

GOD is SO good!

this guy at my job flirted with me and we kissed at the gas station across the street

after we clocked out I invited him

over. He threw me on the ground, raped me, and I fed him

quiche I had made earlier that day after he was conscious again

GOD is SO good!

my dog watched the whole thing and barked until he got too scared

he hid in the corner and continued to watch and after that

he was really fucked up

and wouldn't let men near me, even the ones I told him were good

so I had to give him a better home without bad men or bad me or good me

GOD is SO good!

my brother has never been able to run or jump and he will never be able

to live alone. I get to live

alone and run and jump and I think about how much I want to die

every day

GOD is SO good!

- Ty Little

Home

We crossed the boundaries of three states in five hours

Eating sandwiches out of plastic bags to make the most of our time

Ironic that the only room available was built from the smoke of past occupants

You have bad lungs

The ashtray on the vanity in the bathroom kissed your spine as my hands traced our route from

the road map onto your thighs

We slept among strange sheets curled around one another

Our dreams clung together on our shared pillow, craving familiarity

With the rising sun, we ventured out to meet the mountains

And let the cold air caress your tired lungs

The leaves have become brittle with age

Shedding like flesh onto the earth

We held hands among the skeleton forest

Bark replaced with bone

Three hundred miles from my house, but with your skin touching mine I feel home
- Taylor Allison

A Family Legacy

We carry
abandonment trauma
from one relationship to the next
hoping one day
someone will love us enough to stay,
and we have our parents to thank
for that blueprint.

- Darci McFarland

Trinity

Holy holy holy
three in one, one in three
who says what love can be?
me and him
or him and her and me

Holy holy holy
love in three persons
blessed in trinity
as we disentangle from monogamy

Holy holy holy
him and her and me
celebrate love unconditional and free
where two or more gather
from one we make many

- Layla Padgett

Ransom Note

Kiss my cheekbones;
Rub my stomach.
Apologize
To my mother with your mouth
Against my skin.

She said,
The only way to
Truly scorn g-d
Is to not be thankful.

Touch me with your
Palms
As if you are telling g-d
You are thankful;
touch me
as if you
are scorning
Each gift
By asking for more.

- Luce Grace Kokenge Hartsock

A Texan Drag King's Gender Delight
By Theodore Vegas Zydeco Longlois

At a coffee shop open mic comedy show in Harlem, one of the performers quipped you will never meet a comedian who had a happy childhood or self-confidence. The idea that comedy is born from deep-seated pain and discomfort with oneself bears a striking resemblance to the opening lines of Leo Tolstoy's magnum opus, *Anna Karenina*, "All happy families are alike; each unhappy family is unhappy in its own way." I am definitely not the exception to the stand-up comic's re-interpretation of Tolstoy. As a frequently bullied, chronically ill, queer child of anti-war protesters in South Texas, I often struggled to find a sense of belonging. Yet my stand up as a drag king isn't an act of catharsis. Instead, it's a celebration of a mythical Texas, one where a quirky genderqueer kid gets into wacky hijinks and everything turns out alright.

In many ways, Texas is the embodiment of the United States' colonialism, racism, homophobia, sexism, classism, and ableism. I grew up on ground that had been occupied by at least five separate colonialist and racist governments and was the cause of numerous broken treaties. All for cactus-ridden, mosquito-infested marshland. Today, my friends and family who are people of color live in fear of police brutality, housing and employment discrimination, hate crimes, and the thousands upon thousands of microaggressions which whittle away at their humanity. Their stories are not mine to tell, but I can say I've laid awake in terror many nights after hearing of close calls with trigger-happy police and angry racists. Though my experiences are quite different, I can relate to these microaggressions. Being socialized as a woman, I was taught by teachers, peers, debate judges, church ladies, and random strangers that my opinion didn't matter, that my worth was measured by my modesty, that I should aspire to marriage above all else. Each time I was insulted for appearing less than feminine, each time I was shoved into a locker for being too bold, each time a debate ballot came back with instructions to "break out of my feminine shell," another bar appeared in the cage around my mind. I still wear this cage like a corset, constricting my movements even on the days I attempt to pass as a man. As a queer person, I grew inured to the constant homophobic slurs in the hallways, the way my best friend looked at me in disgust after I came out to her and refused to be alone around me, the prayers for my soul by classmates and church members. But nothing could prepare me for the shooting of two queer girls in a field on the edge of town after a year-long battle to establish a Gay Straight Alliance. Suddenly, home was no longer home.

When I do drag, all this pain and suffering melts away. My drag Texas is a place where my coming out is met with a Texas shaped rainbow cake, not one where I lived in fear my house will be vandalized (or worse) by an ex-boyfriend's angry friends. My drag Texas is a place where my worst day in high school is forgetting to saddle up on the weekly "ride your horse to school" day, not one where the bullying left me feeling broken and unlovable, emotions that kept me trapped in an abusive relationship for years. My drag Texas is one where I worship at the Church of Texas (a church that demands evangelical proclamation of the greatness of the Lone Star State and a multitude of Texas decorations in one's home), not one where my church left the mainstream Presbyterian denomination in protest of the denomination's approval of same-sex marriage.

Yet my drag version of Texas is not entirely revisionistic. My father did bake me a rainbow cake in college, I had incredibly close high school friends who would drop everything if I needed help even 7 years after graduation, and my homophobic church still genuinely cares about me even after I came out. I have spent the last 7 years bouncing between Massachusetts, Alabama, and New Jersey. Living in the North, I began to notice the ways in which the South was more accepting than meets the eye. In Texas, my debate team immediately accepted me when I came out first as bi, then as queer and genderqueer. While a member of the Harvard College Debate Union, I didn't feel this level of acceptance for nearly two years. When I came out to my 83-year-old grandmother, who has lived in the Southwest for all but two years of her life, her response was, "This just shows you love everyone!" When working in Alabama, I had more queer coworkers than I now have queer medical school classmates in New Jersey. In fact, my church circle and activist allies in Alabama espouse more revolutionary generosity than I've seen in any Northern nonprofit. If you look carefully, the coasts are often not as compassionate as one would believe from images of Pride parades, nor is the South as stunted.

On a deadlier note, hate crimes are not only a feature of states behind the Mason-Dixon line. In 2014, two gay men were shot outside a bar near Stonewall. In my experience, Northern racism, sexism, homophobia, and the like percolate behind a polite facade, always two minutes from overflowing. Hatred and discrimination against marginalized groups are a constant feature of life in the

U.S., yet those in "progressive" states are all too ready to see these as relics of a bygone era confined to the backwoods and the bayous.

    I am a firm believer in the idea that comedy, good comedy, should reveal important truths about our society. However, I don't think the truth that discrimination still occurs in the South is the most important truth for my drag to reveal. In a world where those of us from states represented positively in the media and who have the privilege of moving easily see the South as unsavable and refuse to analyze our own prejudice, perhaps the most profound truth is that queer people can thrive in the South. Perhaps the best thing my comedy can do is portray a radically happy Texas drag king.

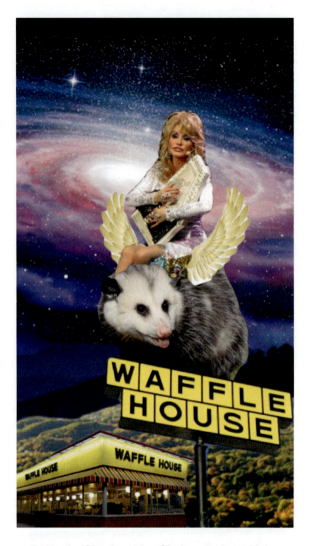

Dolly the Shepherd by Chelsea Dobert-Kehn
Digital collage for Queer Appalachia's onsie fundraiser/ coat drive, Dec. 2018.

[Image Description: Dolly Parton is riding a fluffy winged-sheepdog through a pink and blue galaxy. She has a hitachi magic wand cradled in her arms. In the blue ridge mountains below there is a Waffle House sign.]

Swallowing Light

The flow of sharp heels and rough hands
We drizzled out of Sunday service like a strong current
With staled clothes that hung in the closet
With purpose
When we could only afford one set
For the one day of the week that we could afford rest
What is that feeling we took with us
Out the door
As we drift down the corridor to the light of the day
The mist on the lawn
I see that for some
It is this feeling of flight
Of mercy
Of knowing that Jesus will be in their heart tonight
Of infinite hallelujah
Their bodies only hungry for
Sunday's fresh biscuits & the Holy
My legs tremble in pantyhose
My ankles nervous in white heels that I have scuffed
And dirtied with mud from racing the boys
My heart trembles at His name
Ripples through my baby blue satin dress
That holds me like a cage
I am leaving with a secret that only
Me and Jesus know
And he can't tell anyone
But he is always on my shoulder

That I am the abomination
The part gone wrong
The kind of sinner they had to erect
Walls of worship for on every street corner

A redhead lead me back to her bedroom
Last night
My first taste of queer temporality
When she grabbed my hand in silence
And I knew, the way we've always known our kind
I knew what she wanted from me
Spilled across the bed and I clashed
My skin against hers, to become one flesh
We did what the Bible said we can't
Buzzed on a glass of cheap rosé
Surrounded by antiques and the bouquet of her perfume
The way her mouth met mine
At the precipice of transgressive bliss
In joy & relief, every secret we meant to keep
As friends whose hands lingered too long
Young and doing what we need
In hushed tones and soft sheets
We drifted asleep all wrapped up
In warm light with warm hands
And got dressed at daybreak
The way we always had to then

And I awoke with a funeral in me
I have been to so many of my own
I flowed out to the deck and she
Asked what was wrong
She could not find me when
My eyes were binded in scripture
The glass pupils of a heretic
I looked to the sky for hours
Trying to find my penance
Lord forgive me,
Her hand on my spine felt good
My body raptured by an Auburn saint
And is there no greater sin I'm told
Than this devil in me

That whispered into her soft skin
I waited for the heavens to strike me down
But the skies were too weak that day
I thought if God won't do it
The patriarch in me will do it myself
And save the family name

I flowed into Sunday service
The coming week, sat in the pews
Father, forgive me I will sin again
I know I will sin into her hands
Fall into her soft tendrils of crimson hair
I am no Adam, I know
I just wanted to reach for your creation
And she reached back

Father, forgive me I have fallen from the heavens
And now I got dirt for a soul
Father, I am a tundra
And I need the heat again
The South taught me to burn with joy and elation
So you won't mind if I take this tempered skin
Where I'm going

The book it burns, when I know
God didn't think of me when it got wrote

The organ plays, the choir croons
To hymns that make me want to
Find my weak knees on the ground
in the front of the room
The definition of insanity
With salvation prayers that spill from my mouth
Like an addict in a foxhole prayin' to stay clean
Will these people not teach me to be better

Something worth trying to save
A steely tomboy that could become
A wife someday

All of this to be damned my mother says
He will molt the skin you're living in

I drift from Sunday service yet again
The preachers darting eyes feeling like lead
The redhead across the room looks at me
With eyes that went unfed
I start to think church would be better
With a drink
    And now it reeks

of King James and Jameson
of jaded breath that fills the room
Maybe I can poison a piece of me just yet
The only exor(cis)m I knew
The hymns are softer when I am a lush
The words just drop from me like honey and cream
And darling, it ain't no thing
To be damned for you
These are the sacrifices we make
This is how we queers speak in chivalry
Our equivalent to some man pulling out the seat
How many of us charged the u-haul for eternity

> *Amazing Grace, how sweet the sound*
> *That saved a wretch like me*
> *I once was lost*
> *But now I'm found*
> *Was blind, but now, I see*

My book of Exodus
If I somehow am forgiven

For every morning I woke up entangled
With a body that is fashioned in my image
If all my best parts get hidden
And they call for conversion in the heavens
Electro-shocked halos and they're coming
For the Outlaws of perdition
Who burned The Gospels and told the world about it
If there is no home for our bones, our warmth
Our soul-- in all this dimension then

Who's gonna shut me up in the afterlife
    Who's gonna shut me up in the afterlife

Who?

When I'm still fighting in the end times
When I'm calling on rogue saints
When I am still at odds with it all
And only got 9 shots and defiance left to my name

Who's gonna shut me up in the afterlife

When I'm still smuggling miracles into my pocket

    Swallowing light

To spray back down to my people

   -   Mick McClelland

Genderless Angels

My first fantasy mom crush drove
a white minivan
and brought oranges
to soccer games
with her red hair peaking
behind her bulging eyes
after a sleepover
and several hours of
nonstop talking
in the car ride after
she took me to
her baptist church
and promised
not to return me
with wet hair.

She told me, "my love, you must
accept jesus christ
into your life
as your lord
and savior
or you're going to hell."

She loved me.

My bones said,
My love, love me.
My hole, fill me.
My new mother,
take me in

when its cold
because my mother died
a few years ago
and these bones are hollowing.
My middle-school angst
isn't flowing.
My attempt to find a place
that the boy-girls
are supposed to go
is failing
because there is
only one of us here
and I'm scared.

"My love," she said
 "God made Adam and Eve,
not Adam and Steve."

Twenty years later,
I've been thinking
that Steve was just
Eve's drag name,
the one she gave to herself.
The one she let
wash over herself
before dressing up
and playing sodomy.

What if she just had no other choice?
What if neither of them knew
what a gender was, because
they fucked like animals,

two genderless angels
finding themselves again.

Like when I found myself again.
Like when I began
the process of
standing up straight
when my body
lost part of itself.
When my hunch
from the shame
that she gifted me
as a child
dissipated.

From when the
bible belt smacked me
for having thoughts
outside of normal.
When it showed
what happened to
faggots like me.
When it turned
its nasty head
toward mine
and warned me of
impending doom for eternity.

I didn't know
I would hold her words
like baseball bats
to beat the shit

out of myself
every time I reached
for my partner's hand.
Like daggers for the wicked
Like cuffs for the delinquents
Like hell for the sinners
Like punishment for the miscreants

But I know
nothing feels so holy
as the touch
of their lips to my ear
because, my god.
My god wants
me to fuck like a warrior
To embrace
my queer freak body
like the holy spirit
that it is.
God in flesh.

I want to fuck them
like I've never heard of hell.
I want to fuck them
as if I have always had
the words to describe
this feeling
and I was allowed.
As if someone told me
I could feel this
and be okay
To be more than okay

To be human
To be queer
To be nothing
of gender
and everything of love.

My god, would gasp
and moan
and cry
to their god
to take them home
My god, would get off
when I threw them
against the wall
Held our bad bodies up
to the eternal light of
holy queer gods.
We are power
like the angels
gave to us
to break
this binary down.

As if, she had never
spoke a word to me
Except "my love."
"My love, you are perfect."

- Hayden Dansky

Grounded/Burning by Klée Schell

[Image Description: An orange person is kneeling on the ground with one hand extended in front of them, wearing only socks and underwear. They are equipped with a yellow strap-on, and they have implied healed scars from top surgery. In the image floating near the main figure, there is also a large peach with green leaves, a couple of loosely drawn smiley faces and frown faces, and a link of chain.]

God's Perfect Will by Antonia Terrazas

Original text from "Let's Talk About AIDS and Sex" by Rodney Gage, 1992.

[Image Description: An assortment of carefully arranged items including a Bible, a notebook with the words "queer thoughts" on the front, a coffee cup, and a condom in a gold-colored wrapper subtly peeking out. A book open to a page of text that has been mostly crossed out in black marker, revealing a found poem that reads, "God's perfect will / is misused, abused, and / that will stay with you for a lifetime. / our bodies were meant for / pleasing. / be transformed."]

Battle Scars

By Haden Leevi Britton

I was about 3 years old, running down a dark hallway in the middle of the night in a fit of real terror. I was alone, unsure of where I was running, and the monster chasing me was very real in my young mind. I don't have a lot of memories from this time, but the devastation was hard to erase, though my mind tried. I still have fragments of memory that won't die and others that I cannot reach even if I try. They are still in there, buried, but undoubtedly affecting me. I still remember the sinister face chasing me, like smoldering ash. I felt like this thing could catch me at any moment, and it was enjoying the chase. It was smiling and watching me suffer.

My understanding later became that this situation was my fault. Grownups said it wasn't, but other things they said made me wonder if perhaps the pain of childhood abuse was part of the plan for me. Rather than loathing the planner, I chose guilt. This memory is now something I know to be one of the first times I dissociated. It would be far from the last time. Even today, this is the exact feeling I have when I wake from a night terror or when I drift away into a dark vision, even with others around. It's the feeling of being watched and on the edge of real danger. It is a feeling that you can't trust anything, even your own senses. It's like that monster never really leaves, just waits.

But I had to escape what was happening to me that night, somehow. This must have been the only way my young mind knew to explain the context of my abuse. Later, instead of the religion I was born into coming to save me, I found in various ways throughout my life it added misery and shame. This is not an assault on all beliefs. This is just my truth. I will not skew my emotional experiences with religion for the sake of anyone's comfort any longer. I am going to share things here that very few people in my life know, outside of my marriage and therapy. Vulnerability on this level is terrifying, but I do believe my story matters as much as anyone else's. For the sake of opening minds to an alternative and genuine experience, I will pour my heart onto this page.

Different aspects of identity can fuse together; they interact and are shaped by experience. My major experiences are being queer, growing up in church, growing up poor, a survivor of childhood abuse, and living with PTSD and OCD. Of course, there were plenty of other experiences and memories. Some are brighter than others, and I feel like I've won many battles in the long run. All of these things shaped my life in ways that are profound.

      I am a transgender man living in Oklahoma, and my anxiety in relation to my mental health conditions is extreme. I am a highly sensitive person/empath, and I struggle socially, so I function better one on one, in small groups, or via writing. I experience physical and verbal tics daily and give great effort to suppress them in public since I don't like to be the center of attention. I am currently in the lengthy process of training a service puppy. Her name is Stella, and she gives me a lot of hope, even as she is still learning. I need her help in public, but at this stage, she is primarily helpful to me at home. I mention these things because it is important to understand that trauma and the effort of survival has shaped the person I am today. Some of my trauma has roots in religion. I believe churches are still planting roots like this on a daily basis, whether they realize it or not. And I think that a lot of Christians do realize the harm they've done. For some it hurts too much to admit it. For others it seems like a hobby. Depends on the congregation, I suppose.

      I can remember the pain of religion from early on, when I first learned about good and evil. My earliest recollection would be in a small-town Baptist church, where every Sunday a preacher would go to the front of the room and shout. He was literally vein-bulging, red-faced, shouting bible verses and key messages throughout his speech. He would spit through these fits of livid passion. I was afraid of him, and his presence caused the hairs on the back of my neck to rise. I was also terrified of the devil. Or as most of the church people called it, the enemy. One thing was clear to me even as a small child who could not tie my own shoes, the people who were following the enemy were doing it on purpose and they deserved whatever bad would happen to them. They were fools who chose wrongly. They chose the bad guy, so to Hell with them, literally.

      Also confusing at that age, I never knew which seemingly nice person was working for the enemy full-time. So, I figured I was probably SURROUNDED by the enemy's associates even in church, but **certainly** outside of it. I believe the effect of taking me into that environment each week would be the same as taking a young child into a horror film each Sunday. The conversations disturbed me. Some were based on love and light, but most were based on hellfire and damnation. Children's minds may not generally be best-suited for dissecting complex messages like the ones about how we got here and what our purpose is in this world. I think, kids are meant to be worried about how to catch frogs and countless other things of that nature.

Don't mistake me, kids are intelligent and that's the problem. They must learn so much already. They are sharp and DO try to break down what is being communicated. But they often cannot break down things like metaphors, and there are a lot of gray areas/metaphors in religious talks/texts. At least in my experience, whatever you were saying to me as a child was based on facts. The sky was blue. Bankers were vampires. Elvis was my grandfather (said to me playfully, but I believed it). Pizza was good for me.

This all seemed legitimate enough for me. So if you were going to tell me the enemy was trying to get me, that wasn't poetry to me. That was fact. A physical being was conspiring against my life to trick me into following him so that my God, knowing full well I had been targeted and tricked, would turn his back on me and banish me to the **actual** fiery pits of hell. Check. Got it. I also understood that the enemy lived "down there," understood as below ground. This explains why my little mind, seemingly already coping with OCD, would have me compulsively stomping on the floor to try and get him to go away from me. STOMP! STOMP! STOMP! "Get out of here, Satan!" This was my understanding of reality. Meanwhile, I was told that books about magic and fiction were foolish wastes of time. This all kind of soured the experience of imagination. I mean, we get the Tooth Fairy or Santa, but even then, "He sees you when you're sleeping. He knows when you're awake," sounds a bit threatening once you're focused on Satan, doesn't it?

After a while, I began to interpret religious messages more and more. I was growing so my mind was learning to think critically. It was still difficult to focus for that long each week, and I wanted to play outside. The best I could do was be quiet and not ask for too many drinks or bathroom breaks. But I still absorbed a lot, even when nobody may have thought I was listening. I noticed the preacher was saying "you" to us. For example, "You have forsaken the Lord. You have not been kind. You are not listening to what God needs. You are too busy letting The Enemy control your life." And it hit me with a force that sent me into my first depression somewhere around age 5, the preacher was the good guy and we were ALL the evil fools. Our punishment was to get screamed at every Sunday, and we deserved it! We were bad. One Sunday I innocently asked my mother what we had done this week, so I could prepare for our scolding. I do not recall her exact response, but I remember a shocked look on her face, and I am not certain how much longer we considered ourselves Baptists.

  I admit that I wasn't the easiest child to raise. I already had severe anxiety and was also curious. I would commonly ask my mom to turn a song down to ask questions about the lyrics. I still remember several examples of this. My mom listened to country music. Sometimes what I asked was a bit humorous, "Mom, if all his exes live in Texas, do you think he should date somewhere else?" She laughed and agreed that was a good idea. But sometimes even song lyrics were a bit heavier, "Mom, why does the judge in this town have blood on his hands?" I hated the song with those words because the imagery fueled my nightmares. The concept of a good guy who was really a bad guy. Like those smiling babysitters who hurt me all those years before. I would get this impending doom feeling. I would repeatedly check for monsters, now what I knew to be demons, especially behind the shower curtain because I figured that was the best hiding spot that most people wouldn't think to check. I've always been sensitive in various ways, but spiritually sensitive for sure. I hesitate to share that because plenty of people think that kind of thing is nonsense, and it's their right. But I can confidently say today that the experiences I've known with the other side have been real. They have shaped my understanding of spirituality. Even then, I would stay up late, and I told my mom I couldn't rest because the angels were whispering my name. Again, my best understanding.

  For better or worse, my questions and comments went right to the bone. They still do. I desire truth, and I refuse the notion that religion should not be questioned, especially when there is a connection to tangible personal injury for so many. I know from first-hand experience that congregations are schooled on how to defend their faith against any potential investigation or criticism. Most of the technique seems to be just repeating phrases we have all likely been told. For example, some variation of "God has a reason for everything." This is an incredibly harmful concept when you're talking about being a rape survivor, as one of many possible examples. It was scenarios and statements like this which ultimately made me believe that God felt I deserved the things that had already begun happening to me. To ask someone to believe something and not tolerate or make room for questions and concerns is indoctrination.

Since some of my real experiences were spiritual and positive, I could not release faith in something greater altogether. When I was 7, my grandmother passed away after a long battle with cancer. I knew she left before I was told. I was down the hall and I felt her leave us, like a kiss from the wind. I felt my stomach drop the same way it did at 23 when I found out my best friend died in an accident. My aunt took us next door, and the neighbor asked us what had happened. I said, "My nay-nay died." This was a nickname for my grandma. My aunt was stunned that I was aware of this and I later found out that my grandma actually said someone was there for her and she didn't have time for her coffee now because she had to go. So I always felt connected to the spirit of things and trusted my connection to things I cannot and do not desire to prove. This is why when I talk about questioning religion, I am talking about the religious laws upon others and not about the simple act of believing itself. That feels harmless until it shapes the laws of the land.

I guess it was somewhere around this time that I started being abused again. I could be remembering somewhat out of order since I was so young, but the second bout with abuse triggered the memory of the first. The lines that follow will detail the way I began this essay, talking about my first dissociation in connection to religion after suffering early childhood sexual abuse. Content warning:

I was sexually abused on many occasions, and I recall that over time it escalated. I don't want anyone to have to live with the specific knowledge of this incident that I have, so I will simply say that the abuse was presented as a game that ended with a great deal of physical pain for me in an area of my body that I still avoid as much as possible due to the trauma. This is at the root of why I always feel a step away from danger. The pain was so severe that I left the room, expecting to be chased by my attackers. I didn't know how to get outside. As my fear heightened, I detached. I left myself and watched from above: the tiny feet against the trailer carpet, the darkened shadows of furniture in the living room, the lock I didn't know how to open, the smile of the monster that was about to take part of me forever. The context for the pain was replaced by the vision of this monster (later to be understood as a demon) in the hallway. I kept running, knowing for sure the pain wasn't over and nobody could save me. And nobody did save me. I only made it to the sleeper sofa, where I was left all night alone, discarded. What were the words? What happened to me? If you don't know the words yet, you can't tell. And that's what they were banking on, exactly. The next day they pretended things were normal and were extra kind to me before returning me home with donuts and juice. I felt sick and in shock. They said I was just sleepy. I was so scared of them and their fakeness. I believe at some point they were found out, though my recollection of that part is even more sparse since I was protected from the process. I believe at one point I was told that they were reported to the authorities, and that is all I know. As the conversation about this is exceedingly painful, I don't have plans to ask more information. I genuinely wish them and anyone who hurts children/vulnerable people the absolute worst.

  At that time, I was too young to categorize the events, but as I grew and started to recall the feelings, I coupled them with what I was learning. A lot of what I was learning as a kid was religion. The Enemy brings suffering to his followers, for example. I knew I had suffered. So, I guessed I was born evil. That was a shameful feeling, and I didn't want anyone else to think that about me, so I kept it to myself. And I was still suffering because around the time I turned six years old, I had started to realize that I, assigned female at birth (AFAB), thought that girls were attractive and also had no words to describe that I felt more like my brother than my sister. That is to say, I felt more like a boy who was being told I had to be a girl. I knew that I wanted to play a masculine role in my own life and in my connections. I even knew that someday I wanted to be a husband to someone feminine. I wanted to be poor and thankful for small things with a partner who could find a refuge against my chest. I thought feminine qualities were very attractive but just did not apply to me in many ways. I didn't have a ton of context for a husband because my biological father left when I was very young, but from what I could gather, I wanted to be a good husband. I wanted to be loving, protective, kind, and gentle yet strong. I found out very quickly that the world would not tolerate this queerness.

  It's no secret how religious people often respond to queer sexuality and gender-identities. The minute I was naively bold enough to share my attraction for a girl in class, I was told about how it is wrong to be gay. The Enemy will try to tempt us, but we must resist. I thought, "I can't be evil. I need to be like the good people I know." So, I tried to just not be myself. And what's more, I prayed for God to change my heart. "God, I know it's bad to like her the way I do. I don't mean to. Can you help me to like Timothy instead? I heard he likes me. Please hurry. Amen." Many prayers like this crossed my mind and my lips over the years. Try as I did, nothing seemed to change and I worried constantly if I could do enough good to make up for my identities. Eventually I supposed God couldn't hear me, since nothing had changed my feelings. I did the things the church asked of me. I attended class, camp, vacation bible schools, and more. I feared growing up and making the choice between compromising my identity or owning it and facing what I felt were certain consequences. I was warned that a queer life was a loveless one of pain. But the people saying that were doing nothing to change it either.

Then Ellen DeGeneres came out. I was in grade school. I knew everything that people said about how she was different, mostly insulting things, applied to me. I internalized every single insult. I hated myself very much. Sometimes I still do, especially when I stand next to my little brother and compare. And I must do the work then to love myself and to let us both be beautiful in our own ways. The popular religious and conservative opinion was frequently on the news and still is when we pair religion with politics. They have long not been separate. I remember every time an openly gay person appeared on television and I was told to change the channel immediately because, "This is disgusting and offends God." I had even heard during middle-school that it was customary to "meet God half-way." If you tried to be better, God would help you. So, to do my half, I pretended to like boys and tried to be more feminine. I thought with enough practice, I would eventually get it "right." This didn't work, and I was never good enough at it because it was a lie. My hair was too messy. My clothes were too baggy. And "You look like a boy," was a statement made toward me constantly. I was a boy, after all. But the remark was laden with shame a disappointment. So when I came out the first time in High School, I already knew the way many religious people felt about me. They didn't even need to come tell me directly. Their messages were everywhere and fueled the internalized hate for myself that I already had felt for years. The messages were even at school where I was soon known as a dyke and had bible verses thrown at me regularly. Sometimes I could even spot the disdain in the eyes of some of my teachers. I recall giving an interview for the school paper when a teacher locked eyes with me and said that she believed in "traditional marriage **only**."

I had to learn what I felt was protecting myself, which meant allowing close connections to treat me badly, since I was taught it was just their right to voice their own opinion. It meant trying to prove my love for them, so they might overlook my perceived shortcomings. It even meant making disparaging remarks about who I was. It was a way to beat others to the punchlines, which were many. Making fun of myself was a way for me to air out my learned hatred and shame of who I was. The few times I physically fought in school were to defend others, though in at least one case it was someone who had previously tormented me for years. But I learned to have the foulest mouth and a quick wit against people I didn't know. They could be mean, but I was meaner. It wasn't right, but it was one way of coping. Some would love me. Some would need to fear me. Some would walk all over me. But mostly, people would just stare at me. Afraid to say it out loud now, they'd whisper it and giggle. Adults too. I went few places without groups watching me and this continued until my transition where now my differences are not as quickly noticed. Which is why I'm as out as I can be. Because my beautifully queer and non-binary community won't get a break from the scrutiny. So, I don't want one. I want to knock down these barriers to queer acceptance, love, and health.

Around the time I graduated high school, my rights were all over the news, and to this day they still are. I'm almost 33, and my identity has been under attack in some form for my entire life. It is odd to think about the lives of people who don't turn on the news and see their identities and communities being attacked. For some of us, and not just the LGBTQ+ community, that's all we have known. Most often in my experience, the people who want to take my rights away base their reasoning on their understanding of **religious rule**. I recall when those hateful bigots from a popular Baptist church came to town, just down the street from my home to spread God's supposed hate. They left a vile note on my porch. I threw up.

I recall how other Christians said they didn't like the slurs on those protest signs, but the messages in their politics were always the same to me. If I were to ask why I wasn't allowed to marry someone I loved, the answer was rooted in the Bible. So, did that not mean agreeing with those protest signs? But then they said, "Hate the sin and not the sinner." Oh great, so you don't hate ME specifically, you just hate one major core aspect of who I am as a human? Let me know how that is any better. Don't worry, I will wait. I even wondered why it was THIS particular "sin" everyone was so focused on. But religious people I asked made that simple for me to understand also. See, the difference between me and the other sinners, I was told, was that I CHOSE this as a LIFESTYLE. Meaning that I REFUSED TO REPENT. So, they "worried for my soul." This confirmed what I thought as a child, my soul was considered damaged goods. They offered to pray for my soul. Meanwhile, I worried for my survival on this earth, let alone in what comes after. I never thought I'd live to my 30's. I didn't think I could. I'm so glad I'm still here despite these things.

  In my 20's I realized that I am a transgender man. I also identify as queer because I understand that gender is a construct, and that my identity does not have to obey boundaries set by others. I make my own. For me, this means that I have come to be much more proud of BOTH my feminine and masculine qualities, though I prefer to present myself in a masculine way and to be addressed as a transman, using he/him pronouns. When I transitioned, I had already distanced from the church for about 5 or 6 years. I had met my wife, and at this point we have been together for nearly 14 years, a decade of which was before my transition. I am so thankful that my family grew over all the years, through these very hard things. And though we aren't perfect and they might not even know all of the things I just wrote, I will say that my second time coming out, this time in relation to my gender-identity, was much better. They have tried hard to be supportive, except a few very-religious extended family members who have refused to respect my identity. I have freed them from my presence and myself from theirs. Even though they don't speak ill of my identity and they love me, it's still hard being close to my family sometimes because they still do not hear me when I tell them how the politicians they choose damage my life. They will never understand what it feels like to watch people just like you be mass murdered for being just like you. Just for being. Sometimes I wonder how they can really love me when they don't even understand me. Still, I consider myself fortunate that my remaining family doesn't believe I am going to Hell because many friends have families who still say such things about them. Many have no families at all, save the beautiful chosen ones. My mother is still very involved at church and has defended me to her peers. I admit, it still hurt recently when I went to see her give a speech and I saw a flyer in the building offering to cure "same sex attraction." Someday, I hope that those I love will want to change the religious and political landscape in a meaningful way so that others aren't hurt the way I've been. What can I say, I'm a dreamer.

Religion will always be a problem in my life because Christian extremists shape the law of this land as a weapon to punish people like me. It's like the church arms our government leaders with fear of progress and stubborn refusal to admit that there are so many ways to live this life without harming anybody. These zealots say we are corrupting the children. They say we will ruin the sanctity of their own choices. They say they cannot even associate with us, bake us a cake, allow us to use the restroom, and so much more. They act as if we haven't been here for centuries suffering at the hands of the dominant culture, twisting the narrative so that they are the victims and we are the aggressors just for breathing the same air.

Telling stories like this should not be a brave or dangerous act. But I am often concerned it is both in this environment, which is quickly worsening. This is not hyperbole. Religion has ruined lives and it has been the force behind violence. One may say that's due to perversion of the word, but then I might have to ask which word? Because we know well that those words been interpreted in vastly different ways inside of vastly different churches. And that's only one religion. What of the rest? Understand, safety isn't always physical. I've lost job security over this more than once, with little hope for recourse. People have lost homes and have been denied life-saving healthcare. Queer people have been knocked down over and over, but we keep standing back up. Pride was and still should be a riot until they hear us. Until we remind those straight boys why they don't need a pride. I hope we can all open our eyes and realize that the same prejudice inside of a church moves out on the streets. There are more than wedding cakes at risk here if we continue to allow religious extremists to vilify us. I won't sit idly by. My words are my weapon. My truth is my shield. And I will fight back against being tormented or silenced by religion ever again.

But I'm not an atheist. A part of me survived this journey, underneath all of the emotional scars. The truth is I think often about religion and spirituality, and the way that those are very different things to me now. Religion is something I've parted ways with, for my well being. I don't need a system of laws with skewed interpretations in my spiritual life. We already have that in our government. I just need to believe in the light that fills my spirit and makes me want to keep waking up to love and create. I am thankful to have been able to hold fast to this, even though sometimes I have felt like my spirit was wounded. To me, spirituality can be an amalgamation of faiths and can be something fluid. It admits not knowing all of the answers. It is focused on the self and the connection to a faith in something greater. It can be different for each of us. It can be personal or communal at times, but it requires of one only to recognize connection to all beings on earth and to try to do the most good that is possible.

    I don't want to take away someone's belief system, but I want them to be careful with it. I believe that spirits and emotions are softer than physical bodies, so we need to make sure that the messages we share are not harmful. Commonly when my community voices what is harmful, a response is that we are trying to limit someone else's freedom of religion. But the thing is, we don't care if someone's religion means that they don't like us or the way we live, we can just remove them from our lives. The problem is when people use their beliefs to limit my right to believe and exist in my queer truth. My hope is that people can come to understand that a secular government doesn't ask you to give up your beliefs. It asks you to make your beliefs your own and stop shaming those who live and believe differently. I dreamt a message recently that I think came from someplace important. I'll end with this: "May we do our best along a hellish highway. May we brake when it is safe. May we fight to the finish."

For my grandmother

Along the Treasure Coast we get lots of sun. It's Saturday, laundry day.

My grandmother walks to the laundry room, on the carport.

I head to the bedroom to grab the denim bag off the door knob that leads to her bedroom.

The door that never closes.

We head on to the backyard.

I wear the bag across my body, my grandmother carries the basket.

We start at the far end of the line.

She hangs and I pin, the freshly clean clothes.

If we start early enough we can unpin them by night fall.

In a few years, she will buy a dryer.

I guess eventually we move on.

- Dartricia Walker

Postcard by Sarah Meng

[Image Description: On a back country road in North Georgia an old, two-story farm building somehow still stands, though it has been overcome by time, by rust, by weather. Though the field around the rusted and wooden building has been recently mowed, vines climb up the old building in thick patches. A fence made of wood and chicken wire stands in the foreground among tall weeds. Across the white sky, text added by the artist reads, "This is my home too. I am not always sure how to stay in the south, but leaving her would break my heart. This is my home, too." Underneath the text and to the left of the run down farm building, a hand painted rainbow has been added to the photo. The bright, new colors of the rainbow juxtapose the run down and abandoned farm structure. Text at the bottom of the photograph reads, "Wish you were queer." We have both been here for a long time. The queers, the farm, the plants, the rust. We may be sometimes unsure of how we remain through time and weather, but will all be here for a long time still.]

The Choices I Make
By Leah Whitehead

To: Leah
CC: Beth, Mike, Linda
From: Jim

Subject: Beth's email   Dec 10, 2018, 10:18 PM

Leah, a letter for you after much thought on my part. I have taken the liberty of copying your parents as it was your mothers e-mail that broached the subject. G'dad

Attachment:

Monday, December 10th, 2018

My Dear Leah,

For a week now, I have pondered if and how I should respond to your Mother's e-mail. I now think that I should respond…..
After your relationships with Dave and Jeff, I must say you caught me off-guard. And, since I am several generations out of the mainstream of current thinking and relationships I was sad at the revelation.
Every day we make crucial <u>choices</u> about the basic tenants of our lives:

- Our basic integrity (do we lie, cheat, steal?),
- our relationships (do we gossip, are we true to friends, are we loyal, etc.?),
- our stewardship (God has given us resources…. 'talents', what do we use them for? Do we share with others?, are keepers of others?, leaders or followers, etc.?)
- And yes, even our sexuality. I believe our sexuality is a choice. How do we treat others, both of our sex and the other? What

drives our relationship? Companionship, sex, insecurity, biological, need? What do we want out of the relationship?

I could delve into the Scriptural basics of the Choices we make and I make, but I won't as I don't think you need/want a lecture. Or to be whipped by "What the Bible says….."

So where does that leave me? With your choice….? You know with my background…Christian upbringing, almost 80 years old, conservative, white etc., etc. That I am dismayed. Why Leah?

Please know that I love you deeply. I have watched you mature into a lovely young lady with a heart of gold. I will respect your choices, although I may not agree with them, nor necessarily support them if I think they are to your detriment. That is the case now! But, I do still love you as my flesh and blood and will continue to do so.

Not that you asked, but I thought it important that you know where I stand. It should not change our relationship, but it may.

Please know that I stand ready to discuss your choices or anything else at any time, should you like to.

Fondly,

G'dad

To: Jim
CC: Beth, Mike, Linda
From: Leah

Subject: RE: Beth's email   Dec 11, 2018, 10:09 AM

Attachment:

Tuesday, December 11th, 2018

Dear Granddad and Grandmama,

I've been thinking about writing to you all as well and have been faced with the same conundrum. What do I say? It was no casual decision to tell you all about Liv. I know how you both feel and I knew that this would probably change how you both thought about me. But in the end, the thought of going through one more holiday having to hide an important piece of my life felt impossible and detrimental to my relationship with you all, and with everyone else in our family.

As we move further into this conversation, I want to make sure that we are having the right conversation. Is this about my values? Whether I will spend eternity in hell? About the fact that you feel sexual orientation is a choice? Or that you feel that my choosing Liv as my partner, I am forgoing a healthy relationship built on good morals? The point of this letter is hopefully to give you some more information about the kinds of choices that I am making in my life. I feel confident that we are not going to change each other's minds, so I don't want to waste time on that. I feel like I understand how you feel, and I want to help you understand how I feel too. And then I want to find the best way for us to have a relationship in a way that feels respectful and loving to each other. That will undoubtedly require compromise on both of our parts.

Firstly, I agree that each day we make crucial choices about our lives. Thanks to an incredibly loving and supportive family, I have the privilege of having every tool I need to understand and make those decisions. I consider myself someone of strong integrity. I do not lie, cheat or steal. As I have demonstrated by telling you the truth about who I love, despite the consequence of wading through this discomfort.

I am a loyal friend, a loving daughter, sibling, granddaughter, coworker, mentor, and mentee. I consider my relationships with my given and chosen family to be at the core of who I am. Again why I am choosing to talk through this with you all instead of slowly distancing you until we don't know each other at all, as I'm sure would be much "easier". Not only do I think that relationships are the cornerstones of my personal life, but I truly believe that to spread love and make the world a better place- our best and only tool is the development of compassionate relationships with those we identify with, but especially those we perceive as different from us.

As far as the stewardship of God's gifts to us, I have never sought to be anything but a disciple of love in service of others. I feel called to this life of service, which has led me to the career path that I am on. I recognize that I have been blessed with patience, compassion, understanding and optimism. I feel committed to stewarding those gifts and sharing with others in the spirit of Jesus. Selflessly and in service of those who are most vulnerable in my community.

As far as my sexuality, this is where we diverge. I know that sexuality is not a choice. I've known since I was a teenager that I was also attracted to women. I did not make that choice. Knowing that has let me trust my heart and love people regardless of their gender. Liv is not the first woman I have loved and this is not a new thing or a surprise to me. On this, I doubt we will ever agree, so I don't want to spend too much time on it.

As far as what I look for in a relationship, there are so many things. Mutual respect, deep love and support. Someone who shares my commitment to service, compassion and love, and understands my views on the world. Romantic love. Someone whose goals in life align with mine around creating a family, staying close with my family, and honoring/understanding traditions. Someone who will challenge me to best express myself and steward my God-given gifts in service. Someone who is willing to do the work of communication and long-term commitment. Because I know myself, I have the privilege of falling in love regardless of gender. As I've gotten to know Liv, I have seen all of these things in her and feel lucky to have the opportunity to love her in this way.

Our relationship is not driven by need or insecurity, but by mutual love and trust. How beautiful and rare! I feel overjoyed to have found such a partner.

I'm happy to share the scriptural basis on my life choices. Specifically on the choices I make and their consequences on the world and on others. To me, my choice to love live is not in contrast to the teachings of Christ. In fact, I believe

God loves me exactly as I am and knows the extent to which I seek to exemplify Him in my work, my family, my community, and yes, my relationship.

I don't argue that there are pieces of the Bible that condemn homosexuality. But upon taking the book as a whole and considering the teachings of Christ in context of their time, I feel certain that the core take away is Love, Service, and Discipline. Not don't be gay. Considering the consequences that my choices have on others, I also feel as though loving Liv has consequences for very few other people besides myself and her.

So what now?

My impression from you all is that the best-case scenario is that I feel ashamed or awakened by your words, confess the temptation/brainwashing that has led me to homosexuality to you and God and promptly fall into a strictly heterosexual, Christian lifestyle, feeling closer to God and to you all because of it.

For me, the best-case scenario is that you all realize that I am joyful and loved and fulfilled by my relationship with Liv. That you pray and talk to God and realize that He loves me exactly as I am and knows what is in my heart better than you or I. In that scenario, I feel loved and supported by you all and you get to know Liv the way you would welcome any partner of mine, with love and open arms.

I'm under no illusions that either of us are going to get exactly what we want. Here we are again, presented with yet another choice. I see a few options, and are open to hearing any more you can think of.

a) You may get this letter and feel further dismayed. You may feel angry or disappointed and decide to continue sending me variations of your thoughts in the form of scripture, moral lectures, or otherwise. Following this I might feel so nervous to see you at Edisto because I'm afraid you will continue telling me how disappointed you are or, worse, condemn Liv or myself. In this situation, I can imagine leaving Edisto feeling unwelcome and unloved and not wanting to return. This would be so hard, not only on our relationship, my relationship with the rest of our family, but also on my Mom and your relationship with her.

b) You may get this letter and feel frustrated, but resigned. We could plan to talk at Edisto when I'm there, to clear the air and say whatever feels unsaid. At that point y'all might drift into polite distance/ disapproval. Occasionally making comments about my 'choice', or sending passive emails/messages about it. As you said, you think this is to my detriment and do not support it. I anticipate that wouldn't feel very good and may also make it difficult to look forward to seeing you all because there would always be this undertone of discomfort, but maybe we wouldn't have to interact with it that much and it would be fine since everyone else has been really supportive.

c) You may get this letter and be reminded, as I hope you are, that I have been raised in the path of Christ and carry those values in my heart. You may be able to reckon with the possibility that this will not send me to Hell and be reminded that I am being thoughtful. Maybe you still choose to keep me in your prayers in this way, but ultimately see that I am happy, safe and healthy- which is such a blessing. In this scenario, I may mention Liv as I talk about my adult life with my family and it might make you uncomfortable, but you don't feel the need to make comments about it. We continue on, somewhat similar to before. Seeing each other at family holidays, sending loving messages on special occasions, and visiting each other when possible. Eventually in this scenario, Liv might be welcomed to Edisto for a family Holiday, and would be welcome when y'all are not there.

d) You may get this letter and see that this is not a situation ruled by political opinion or belief, but a choice about our relationship that we can make. We could be presented with the opportunity to call a draw, and follow the words over another family member, whose response to my coming out was, "You do you, and be happy." In that scenario I would proceed exactly the same as I would if Liv was a man. Talking about her openly and inviting her to family events when possible. Maybe even looking forward to sharing time with the four of us, such as you have been able to do with Austin and Ainslie.

I've watched a lot of people with conservative family members handle this situation. So many of whom don't talk to their families anymore because they were bombarded with messages that were hurtful. I don't want that to happen. And yet...

My reality is that I love Liv and that is not a sin, but a celebration in the eyes of God.

Your reality is that I love Liv and that is a detriment to my spiritual and eternal health.

Woof, what a hard thing to navigate!

It is hard enough for me to know what you think about my relationship, yet alone be reminded of it constantly. I hear you say that you love me, but it does not feel like love. I am prepared to continually and actively seek to understand and trust that you love me in your own way. I know that it is part of your belief system that you have a responsibility to change how I live my life. But I also know that it is going to be really hard for me to upkeep our relationship if you are constantly feeling the need to do that.

So what do you think? Do you see other options? I have so much optimism that love will win. That you might see that what God wants is for us to love and support each other and live lives in the spirit of Christ, which we both do in our own way.

If it is okay with you both, I think we ought to not talk more over email, but to take the next couple of weeks to pray on this and consider what we both need to move forward towards an outcome that feels okay to both of us, whether considered here or something else entirely. I'd love to know that you read this. Feel free to send a quick, got it! Just to let me know, but no pressure to respond otherwise.

I look forward to sitting with you both over the Holidays and talking more. Know that I love you both very, very much and am committed to figuring this out with you.

All my love,
Leah

To: Leah
CC: Beth, Mike, Jim
From: Linda

Subject: RE: Beth's email   Dec 11, 2018, 10:39 AM

I did get it, Leah, and I do love you no matter how it looks to you.
Grandmama

Sent from my iPad

To: Leah
CC: Beth, Mike, Linda
From: Jim

Subject: RE: Beth's email   Dec 11, 2018, 11:11 AM

Well said! I am not sure this discussion is the way I want to spend our holidays. We'll see. Grand dad

Contours
By Jean Thomas

I'm so nervous I stay in the driver's seat for a few extra minutes, letting the chair recline further and further back. *Maybe I don't have to go in?* I've been talking myself through the slow creep of anxiety all day and up until now, I've been edging out the paranoia just slightly. Sometimes being a therapist is agonizing—I know the thing I need to heal and still fight it anyway.

I try to remind myself why I'm here, parked up the street from the Women's Center. I think of Deborah and the guilty feminist army. I think of how she's built her hope on the swords half drawn. I need to work with women who are ready to build. I need to look into their eyes and see the worry I carry around. I desperately need to draw lines around the life I don't want and find the contours of the one I do. And yet my anxiety would rather I just turn the whole operation around and leave. *What is it that really scares me, honestly? Is it who I might find inside? Am I afraid that I'll walk in and discover that safety isn't really possible here either? What if I've imagined women to be my saving grace and they wreck me again?*

I take a few deep breaths, letting the worry settle until it's less boisterous. *That's a little dramatic, isn't it? It's just a women's center, not a courthouse with the power to banish you from the sisterhood forever. Though, now that I think about it, I'm a feminist, and I sort of wish we did have a Supreme Court. Nine ladies and femmes that comment on our pedagogy and decide what's best for the collective?* That sounds more reassuring than this—just clusters of women and genderqueer people trying to write ourselves out of patriarchy and into the freedom we dream up.

I square my shoulders a bit, look over at the passenger's side and spot the leather jacket on the seat rest. *Perfect.* I slip off a sweater that's never quite fit and into the kind of hard leather I feel at home in. I run my hand through buzzed hair and down toward the base of my neck. The muscles are tenser than I thought they'd be.

I think about the second wave when were booed out of auditoriums and conferences. I think about how we stood up anyway, our lavender chests peaking through and announcing themselves. I wonder if we felt like wearing queerness made us braver. *Why are women always signaling to each other in fabric? Why do clothes need to stand in for armor? Can't we read each other properly without it?* I wonder how I'll find a way to be vulnerable once I'm inside. *Are there more people like me out there? Are we all just worried about walking into the unknown and finding ourselves in some kind of closet?*

I slowly raise the chair back up and propel my spine to sit straighter. I pop open the drivers side door and throw one leg onto the street. I'm about to swing the other over when I see the home screen on my phone light up. It's a picture of Kerry Washington from last year's Women's March. She has her fist up in the air, hair pulled back into braids.

I still remember that day, watching her lead the crowd in a kind of prayer. There she was, overlooking a sea of largely white faces, peeking through bright pink hats. There she was, standing firmly in the truth of what she needed to say, trying to outline the contours of us. She opened by imploring everyone to see ourselves as part of an ongoing, broader struggle for justice. Invoking the image of Olivia Pope and explaining how many on twitter had called on her, a fictional character, to fix this moment for them, she asserted that black women are not here to challenge the patriarchy for us. She called on marginalized people to remember how much we matter—if not to America, then to each other. She said "We the People" means us—the us who have been shut out of democracy for generations.

She also closed with this: "in those moments when I am scared and alone, I have to remember this 750,000 strong. We have to remember that we have each other and that we are going to hold hands and make it through." When I heard this for the first time, I wondered if in those moments of fear, she calls on a sea of faces that remind her of family. I wondered if in her mind the 750,000 strong walk in the footsteps of Fannie Lou Hamer and Rosa Parks, Marsha P Johnson and Audre Lorde, bell hooks and Brittney Cooper. I wondered what it would take for the sea of faces to follow a black feminist blueprint, to dream of a similar We the People.

She seemed to be imagining that a messy, imperfect coalition was possible, that we could all refuse to bargain with the freedoms of others in pursuit of our own. That generosity of spirit, the kind that looks history in the eye and chooses to believe in the possibility of justice, moved my spirit someplace steadier.

Every time I see that picture of her, I think of what she offered that day to a sea of faces that looked like mine: to know how often white women have buoyed ourselves with false promises of patriarchs, unwilling to reckon with the livelihoods we'd comprise in the process; to know the violence of that history and still insist that democracy can be righteous? To know that history and insist that We the People can be transformed, solidified into more than an empty promise?

I don't know how she experienced that moment on stage, or whether she's felt like we've answered her call since. What I do know is that white women cannot clamor for "unity" without addressing how we made all-of-us-together feminism impossible in the first place. What I do know is that us isn't something we can claim—it has to be earned back. What I do know is that the work can't look like re-centering ourselves at the expense of other bodies. We've turned us into only us—only boardrooms, only leaning in, only pussy power, only traumas we can recognize ourselves in.

As I get ready to step out of my car and onto the street, I think of Kerry's prayer and I think of mine: how can I push white cis women to expand the lens beyond our own pain? How can I walk through the fears that keep me from finding the us I need, from challenging that same us to do better?

I take a deep breath and pull my body into the open air. I exhale, nowhere near steadfast. I remember Deborah and the guilty feminists. I remember the world we're fighting for. I remember the call to arms I sometimes repeat on hard days:

Black lives matter

Every body belongs to itself

Queer love is revolutionary

Survivors deserve love and safety

Women are more than the history we carry

Gender has never been binary

Sisters can be more than cisters

Self-care is not self-indulgent,

neither is dreaming.

I shut the car door and slowly walk up to the front entrance. I go to grab the door knob and see a sign that reads: "Step right up. We've been waiting for you. You're welcome anytime." *Time to find the contours of us.*

Confessions of a Pentecostal Queer
By Amanda L. Pumphrey

Growing up in the rural South is similar to living in rural communities outside of the Southeastern United States. Everyone has to drive an average of 30-50 miles to get to the nearest shopping mall or hospital. Traffic jams are only caused by enormous mobile farming equipment or cargo trains passing through the towns. There are distinguishing factors that are unique to specifically growing up in the South, and by South, I mean the DEEP South. As in so far south that my next door neighbor's dog was eaten by a massive 13 foot alligator. So Southern that as a child I watched in sheer terror from the back pew as my teenage babysitter was exorcised of slut demons in front of the entire congregation on what I thought would have been just a typical Pentecostal Sunday service with only mild amounts of speaking in tongues and the laying on of hands. Give me that old time religion, indeed. My South is a particular and peculiar context. One in which I witnessed a youth pastor physically break Billy Blanks' Tae Bo video tapes because they were of the devil; a context in which my biological family was the epitome of stereotypical and hypocritical white-uneducated-redneck-bible-thumping-holy-rollers. I was considered the Black Sheep because I was different on multiple levels but I was also Queer.

Flash forward nearly two decades later and I am in Kansas City, Missouri getting a tattoo of a Femme alliGAYtor riding a rainbow wave. This statement piece is one of the ways I chose to visibly embrace my seemingly contradictory positionality as a Pentecostal Cuntry Queer Millennial. I cannot confirm if all Southern Queer Folks have these experiences, but there are many commonalities that we share. Once we look beyond our initial communities, we notice how those outside of the South are utterly confused by us and how their harmful stereotypes erase the diversity and nuances of Southern Queerness. After several years of self-loathing, followed by continual (un)learning, building my chosen family, and constant mental processing because I am a Virgo Sun and Capricorn Moon; I accept myself in relation to the complex, complicated, extremely painful and traumatic context in which I grew up. After living outside of the Deep South for over a decade on the West Coast and the Midwest, it took experiencing the myriad of ways I have been (mis)read and treated to understand the nuances of my identities and be-ing as directly connected spiritually and spatially to a place.

Throughout my youth, I was not only extremely embarrassed that I was different as a closeted teen struggling with their gender and sexual identities; I was also deeply ashamed that I was Pentecostal. Within my church community, I was both an outsider and an insider. I was often shamed for never publicly receiving the Holy Spirit. I was never "filled" with the Holy Ghost, and I never "spoke" in tongues. This was extremely taboo for Pentecostals and especially within my extended biological family which consisted of Pentecostal preachers and church musicians. I was always made to feel that something was inherently wrong with me. I was not fully opening my heart and mind up to Jesus. I was not praying enough. I was not reading and studying the Bible enough. I was not enough.

One summer I nervously invited a friend who was not Pentecostal to attend Pentecostal Jesus Camp with me. I was surprised they agreed and that their parents allowed it. I was very much aware of how my peers from the county public school viewed Pentecostals. Many of them were from wealthy families who attended the fancier, brick churches located downtown. They did not have to travel several miles out of town into the country, driving down the red clay dirt roads in order to attend service at a small, backwoods church. Where you never knew exactly how long you would be there depending on how the Spirit moved. The Holy Spirit would move the choir director causing the choir to sing for nearly 2 damn hours. Bless their hearts because you know they were exhausted and distracted while the congregation was shoutin', runnin', jumpin', and rollin' around on the floor, drunk in the Spirit. The Holy Ghost could fall over a congregation member who then received the gift of faith healing. Everyone who had an ailment would come forth to be anointed with oil and prayed over. Years later I realized that the so-called anointin' oil just so happened to be the cheapest brand of olive oil from the local Piggly Wiggly. Gradually, I began to notice the way non-Pentecostal denominations viewed Pentecostal churches and how the intersections of race, class, and socio-economic status functioned in their disdain towards rural Pentecostalism.

Since I started driving and working part-time jobs when I was in high school, I had given up on fitting in within my church community. I was too much of an outsider at this point. Even though I still was silently struggling with understanding my gender and sexual identities, I began to hold space for those feelings and I started to become more aware and intentional in my views and actions. I wrote my high school senior paper on my support of marriage equality which was a highly controversial issue in the current Georgia state elections. I had stopped going to Wednesday night youth group. I had stopped going to every Sunday service as well. I was what I now look back and call "softball straight." I was obsessed with my short hair, womxn's sports culture, and my 1978 Trans Am. I was fascinated by what I now recognize as explicitly Queer Culture & Aesthetics, but then I was too afraid to admit it. Much like how I felt like an outsider / insider in my church community, for a long time I felt the same way within the Queer Community as someone who does not neatly fit in as a Queer Bisexual Non-Binary Femme.

  Growing up in a Southern Pentecostal context forced me to cultivate a deep shame of any form of femininity because it was always perceived as lesser and weak, which also made me ashamed of my sexuality. The fact that I could be both femme and a sexual being with agency and autonomy seemed completely impossible. Many of the youth group sermons that I sat through with my Poker Face were about the temptation of sin through sexual desires and the pure evil of sex before marriage. The feminized temptresses were always to blame. I thought this is why I could never receive the Holy Spirit; I was too sinful at my core. My very existence was the ultimate abomination because I was Queer and Femme. My body, my presence, my thoughts, my feelings, my complete be-ing was the embodiment of sin. These beliefs slowly started to change as I actively made the decision to stop attending services, moved away to college, and began to (un)learn toxic theology through becoming a Philosophy and Religious Studies major focused on gender and sexuality. Being "smart" and receiving scholarships was my ticket out of my hometown. Initially, I bought into educational elitism and I never imagined the negativity I would receive as a first generation college graduate from the rural South during my M.A. and Ph.D. programs in Los Angeles County, CA at private universities. I was told that I needed speech therapy to lose my thick Southern accent. A professor told me I would not be taken seriously as a scholar with an accent that holds such negative political and stereotypical implications. Once after I presented a paper, a colleague stated that they loved my accent but it was so distracting they did not understand my point. At a conference I was asked if I had ever been treated for worms because I was Southern. While I was constantly othered for my Southernness, my gender presentation and my queerness was always in question as well. I often allowed my queerness to be erased and misread because I was already immediately targeted as soon as I spoke. I continued to be both outsider / insider as I transitioned back and forth between returning to the South, being in graduate school in L.A., and going to queer events and bars with friends. After moving to Kansas and teaching undergraduate courses on gender and sexuality, I have felt yet another shift in my be-ing. I made some of the best friends, who are now my family, outside of graduate school because they did not otherize me, fetishize me, or only treat me as their competition. Several of my dear friends are also Queer Transplants, Rural Queers, and Queer Southerners. I love all of our uniqueness and diversity of experiences that we can share with one another. Finding Online Queer Communities has also been extremely comforting and important as I am in a liminal space of The Middle.

I am still healing from my traumatic upbringing and the toxicity of academia in order to reclaim what it means for me to be rural, Southern, Pentecostal, and Queer. I will never attend a Sunday church service again, and I will never receive the Holy Ghost by certain standards. Going to Church is when I witness my Beloved friends performing their art, drag, and music. Tithing is $upporting Queer artists-activists-academics' work. I feel the presence of the Holy Spirit when I am with my best friend blasting Lady Gaga driving down the 10 freeway on the way to West Hollywood. I received the Funky Queer Spirit at The P.U.S.C.I.E. Jones Revue shows. I felt the Divine Power of Queer Womxn & Femmes when we were gathered together in numbers at Syd's Always Never Home Tour in downtown Los Angeles. Attending Kansas City Pride and Chicago Pride is like visiting a brand new church and feeling at home. Reading @QueerAppalachia and @QueerNature posts are my Sacred Scriptures. Sunday School is when I teach students that the binaries upheld by white supremacist-cishetero-patriarchal christianity must be broken. I am a Pentecostal Preacher in my own right, filled with the Queer Holy Spirit. Now, I speak with authority in my undeniably thick Southwest Georgian Accent, in my Pentecostal Queer Tongue, so All Y'all can hear me loud and clear: I am Southern. I am Pentecostal. I am Bisexual. I am Non-Binary. I am Femme. I am a Bible Belt Queer. *I am.*

Community by Darci McFarland

Community by Darci McFarland

[Image description: Community is a mixed-media spread that showcases a messy watercolor rainbow background with conversation bubbles scattered throughout that feature quotes from contributors & supporters. The quotes read:

- "I hope that we as southern queers become more visible to those outside our community who think we all jump ship for the north at 18."
- "I will not give up on the South, or the Southern parts of myself and my queerness."
- "I pray that some young person gets ahold of my poem and sees hope there."
- "When my friend showed me the request for submissions I remember thinking, 'this is just what I need, what WE need as queer religious people.' This process has made me feel so connected in a place where I did not know I could find connection. It is a joy to find myself in the pages of so many beautifully empowered and brave people - I am hoping my art can reflect this."
- "I'm a 60 year old bisexual who grew up in TN & lives here now. We need as much representation of LGBTQ+ Southern folks as we can get. Thank you!"
- "It's been refreshing to see the amount of queer creativity being brought together all in one place. I feel a sense of community being involved in this collection and speaking such honesty in my poetry about someone of the same gender."
- Sometimes I feel alone in my battle with accepting my sexuality & standing up for myself against such strong familial, religious opposition."
- "The work you're doing is so vital to our collective healing. Thank you!!"
- "This process reminded me that my positionality as a bible belt queer matters and has something to say in the larger conversation on queerness."
- "I think about how deeply I needed this anthology when I was first coming out. My experience of queerness has been intimately & inextricably intertwined with my spirituality/religious experiences. Where else has this been explored?"
- "Thank you for lifting up queer voices in an area it is so needed."
- "This was my first time submitting work, and I was nervous. Afterward, I can't stop thinking about being a part of more projects and even taking on my own as an individual. It has been a trans-formative experience. I'm deeply impacted knowing that my voice will be heard. I tell myself this project will find its home where it is needed most. I needed this book when I was younger. I need it still."]

Made in the USA
Monee, IL
20 December 2019